THE
UNOFFICIAL®
Disney
Companion

GW00361979

Also available from Macmillan Travel:

THE
UNOFFICIAL®

Disney
Companion

**The Inside Story of
Walt Disney World®
& the Man Behind
the Mouse**

Eve Zibart

Macmillan • USA

Macmillan Travel
A Simon & Schuster Macmillan Company
1633 Broadway
New York, New York 10019

Produced by Menasha Ridge Press
Design by Barbara E. Williams

Macmillan is a registered trademark of Macmillan, Inc.

The Unofficial Guide is a registered trademark of
Robert W. Sehlinger

ISBN 0-02-861557-3
ISSN 1089-8050

Manufactured in the United States of America

10 9 8 7 6 5 4 3 2 1

CONTENTS

- **Afterword:** "Mirror, Mirror, on the Wall . . ."   191
- **Appendix:** A Brief History of the World   195
- **Index**   215

ACKNOWLEDGMENTS
AND DEDICATION

$\mathcal{T}$his book would not have been possible without the assistance of many sources, both on and off the record, and on and off the Web. My gratitude.

I am especially grateful for the professional courtesy of the *Orlando Sentinel,* the newspaper that made Walt Disney World possible in the first place. The *Sentinel* has striven ever since to make sure the company lived up to its promises. Its archives were invaluable.

Thanks as always to the folks at Menasha Ridge Press, especially Bob, Molly, Holly, Patt, and Mary Ellen.

My warmest thanks, however, go to Heather Freeman and Stuart Freeman, who not only opened their home to me as a base of operations and tolerated my stress jags and long hours (and covered me with comforting animals), but who gave me reason to remember that the most magical kingdom is the one your friends' affection constructs around you. This book is for them.

—*With love, Eve*

PREFACE

Welcome to the World

*T*he night before Walt Disney died, he called his chief of operations, Admiral Joe Fowler, to the hospital. Lying in his bed, Disney pointed to the ceiling, and on that blank white "sheet," he drew his dream park's layout, its shape, its flow. "As ill as he was," Fowler told the *Orlando Sentinel* more than 20 years later, "he acted like a boy just let out of school. The last draft of what is now Disney World was sketched out, figuratively, on that ceiling. And the next day, he died."

Most castles in the air are never built. But Walt Disney's was, and it became the symbol of one of the most successful corporate kingdoms ever created— one worth an estimated $50 billion. But it wasn't always the park Walt envisioned, and its "last draft" is far from finished.

This is not a tour guide to Walt Disney World; it does not replicate *The Unofficial Guide to Walt Disney*

World, its companion volume that evaluates every ride and tells you how to get the most out of your time at the park. It is neither exposé nor promotional brochure. Instead, this is a book for the armchair traveler, the repeat customer, or the trivia fan—a reader's companion to the largest, most opulent, fascinating, and vital theme park in history.

This is a different kind of stroll through Disney World: part history, part myth, part whodunnit and how. It's a mixture of intuition, interpretation, and investigation. It's a look at the nuts-and-bolts of a few rides (everything but the whirl), the amazing facts and fictions of the landscaping (the roots of the problems), the grown-ups' attractions and bars (Is there a new sort of "mickey" in the works?), and a few real-life hazards (what it's like to be the mouse behind the mask). It's not the final word on the park—that may never be written, considering how many new hotels and attractions are constantly being constructed—but it should answer some of your questions and give you something to pass the time while you're standing in line for Space Mountain.

As Disney itself has reminded us, Beauty is in the eye of the beholder—and so is the Beast. So this book mixes kudos and carping. We raise some cultural qualms about the treatment of women, blacks, and other minorities in the park's attractions, but we also applaud some of the policies toward minority employees of the company. We shake off some of the "pixie dust," perhaps, but the business savvy and the scientific and technological glitter are far more impressive—and so are some of the shortcuts, in their own way.

And we consider the Kingdom's two rulers: Walt Disney himself and crown prince Michael Eisner, at once Walt's opposite and his natural heir. The building, and the rebuilding, of Walt Disney World and the Disney Company is a Hollywood story in its own right, full of intrigue, dummy companies, big budgets, family squabbles, Wall Street jitters, and record-breaking grosses.

And we can't forget the magic, of course. After all, "magic" is the kingdom's middle name.

Walt Disney World

535

535

Osprey Ridge
Golf Course

Bonnet Creek
Golf Club

Live Oak
Lane

Buena Vista Drive

Eagle Pines
Golf Course

Vista Blvd.

Community Dr.

The Crossroads
Shopping Ctr.

Dixie Landings
Resort

Disney Village
Conference Ctr.

Travelodge
Hotel

Port Orleans
Resort

Doubletree
Guest Suites

Disney
Institute

Buena Vista Palace

Old Key
West

Disney's Village Resort

Grosvenor
Resort

Hotel Royal
Plaza

EXIT 27

Bonnet Creek Rd.

Lake
Buena Vista
Golf Course

Disney
Village
Marketplace

Courtyard by
Marriott

535

The
Hilton

Pleasure Island

Typhoon Lagoon

To Orlando

Caribbean
Beach Resort

EXIT 26

4

536

EXIT 25

To Tampa

Osceola Parkway

192

To Kissimmee →

INTRODUCTION

A View of the World

*T*he story goes that author Ray Bradbury, himself a fairly sophisticated prognosticator of socioscientific advances, was so dazzled by the original Disneyland that he asked Walt Disney to consider running for mayor of Los Angeles. Disney, after a moment's thought, supposedly responded, "Why should I run for mayor when I'm already king?"

The Magic Kingdom may have been Walt's crowning achievement. But Walt Disney World, the house the Mouse built, is far more influential now, a whole generation after its opening, than Walt could ever have dreamed. Walt Disney World has not only transformed the entertainment industry, but has pushed the envelopes of visual and electronic effects, psychological packaging, and land management—and has put a serious dent into the nation's impression of its own history.

The theme parks that most people see are only a

fraction of the whole World, not only in the physical sense (the Magic Kingdom alone has nine acres of "basement"), but financially, politically, technologically, and sociologically. It is a fascinating amalgam of capitalism, free enterprise, socialism, artistic patronage, "green" politics, and rigid, one might almost say "Red," employee rules.

When it comes to talking money, Disney dollars are metaphorical gold. The phrase "hundreds of millions" scarcely even applies anymore. As pointed out in "Pleasure World: Disney for Adults," the company has spent perhaps $400 million on sports acquisitions, franchise bids, and facilities over the last three or four years. More than a billion dollars' worth of new hotels and attractions are in some stage of construction. Celebration, the model town of 20,000 residents that Disney has built in Osceola County, cost $2.5 billion. But even that pales in comparison to the $19 billion deal Disney made in August 1995 to purchase the Capital Cities/ABC television network company.

Billions in, billions out. The value of Disney stock has increased more than 1,000% since Michael Eisner became chairman in 1984, and *New Yorker* media critic Ken Auletta estimates the total value of the Walt Disney Company at $50 billion.

Walt Disney World is its own city-state: officially, the Reedy Creek Improvement District, an entity as self-sufficient as its predecessors of the Italian Renaissance, and bigger than some. (Some Florida officials have referred to it as "the Vatican.") It has its own tax-ing authority and the power to issue bonds; it makes its own zoning decisions and sets its own building codes, which are actually stricter than those of most other American cities. It supplies and maintains all power for Walt Disney World, producing about 25% of it within the Reedy Creek District itself and buy-ing the rest. It has its own Environmental Protection Department. It issues its own building permits, and its bottom-line attitude toward labor and construction has allowed the company repeatedly to meet what seemed to be impossibly short deadlines. The taxes it levies pay for utilities, roads and infrastructure, fire protection, and public transportation within the dis-trict; the taxes it pays Osceola and Orange counties (the Disney tract straddles both) go for police, educa-tion, and welfare services.

The company's progressive—or pre-emptive, de-pending on your viewpoint—dealings with labor unions is the envy of other municipalities. In 1969, during the construction of Walt Disney World, a 3-year agreement involving Disney and the AFL-CIO prom-ised that in the case of contractual disagreements, a neutral umpire would be called in within 24 hours to issue an immediate decision if the local unions agreed not to strike, picket, or stop work until the project was complete. And to make sure the project was overseen by someone with hands-on experience, Disney hired Major General William Everett "Joe" Potter, an MIT-trained Army chief engineer, former governor of the

Panama Canal Zone, and second-in-command of the New York World's Fair.

The internal structure of the park and its attractions are the envy of urban planners as well. Most of Walt Disney World has been designed by artists and engineers called "Imagineers," who create the attractions from inside out—that is, starting with the show, then sketching the theater, and then the architecture itself—rather than always beginning with square footage and configuration. Disney engineers developed an innovative system of water reclamation to prevent either flooding or excessive drainage, continual threats in the central Florida wetlands; and Disney World was the first United States property to install a fully automated vacuuming and compacting trash collection system that uses pneumatic tubes.

Its telecommunications company, a joint venture of Disney and United Telecommunications, produced the first fully electronic telephone system (with all underground cable), the first commercial fibre optic system for voice in the country, and one of the first computer-controlled systems; in 1985, it became the first telephone company to go completely digital. It has a satellite system/cable TV network; a private "red line" satellite hook-up to Walt Disney Productions in California; and an interactive audio/video information system throughout EPCOT that provides directions, background, routes, and updated schedules for the entire park.

But it isn't just the technology or politics of Walt

Disney World that make it interesting; it's the World's role in our world, its peculiar and frankly prettied-up view of American culture. Anthropologist Stephen M. Fjellman, in his landmark and somewhat rococo study, *Vinyl Leaves: Walt Disney World and America,* takes a sort of modified Marshall McLuhan approach to Walt Disney World: The medium is the message is the marketing.

Fjellman is concerned that we recognize Walt Disney World as a "commodity," a product being prepared for mass consumption, and he wants visitors to be aware of the underlying messages—in some cases, biases—being perpetrated by certain attractions. Fjellman calls it "the most ideologically important piece of land in the United States . . . the quintessence of the American way," because it has not only perfected the balance of nostalgia and personal accommodation but has assembled a huge network of media tie-ins, button-pushing hype, and marketing savvy to make sure the nostalgia continues to sell.

Fjellman says that Walt Disney World has captured "the symbolic essence of childhood" as opposed, presumably, to an actual experience. It combines memories from images either seen in fact or "borrowed" from cultural artifacts (just the sort of bowdlerized nostalgia that permeated Disney movies in the old days as well). He points out that much of the experience is physically passive—he sees the overall structure as cinematic, a "you are there" in 3-D—and that most of our responses are not only carefully orchestrated but built into the actual design in terms of timing of special effects and so on.

He also points out that in its immaculate cleanliness, its strict-to-the-script casting, its crime-free and car-free Main Street, and its almost religious anti-littering and anti-pollution design, Disney World provides an *apparent* antidote to the fears, the increasing isolationism, and the professional–personal fracturing of everyday life. It is a sort of Oz at the heart of Kansas, he says, and like all Ozes, it has a would-be wizard (in this case, hundreds of them) pulling strings behind the curtain. Where most of us see Cinderella Castle, Fjellman sees Fritz Lang's *Metropolis,* the luxury above coming at the expense of the utility corridors and concession carts and service workers laboring underground.

Unlike a lot of Walt Disney World's critics, Fjellman has spent a great deal of time at the park and is genuinely fond of it despite the valid questions it raises. Other observers have raised similarly valid criticisms, including the fact that over a period of years, by adding additional theme areas and self-contained sports complexes and hotels, Walt Disney World has attempted to monopolize not only the theme park consumer but the entire entertainment dollar.

Yes. It's all true, good and bad. Minorities and women are given appallingly short shrift in even the latest re-edited versions of *The American Adventure* and *The Hall of Presidents* audio-animatronic shows. On the other hand, Disney has also provided insurance benefits to same-sex partners (an act for which it has taken hits from conservative groups); closed the gates for the annual Gay and Lesbian Day in June, which attracts an estimated 60,000 guests; and refashioned its old Universe of Energy program as a vehicle for gay comic Ellen DeGeneres, whose show is on the Disney-owned ABC. The company has been both intent and imaginative when it comes to expanding its fiscal base, taking on corporate co-sponsors, beating competitors to the promotional punch, and especially catering to the increased spending power of the over-35 generation.

It's also fair to emphasize the blinkering effects of such total-package marketing. But something more ornate than mere symbolism is operating here. Walt Disney World reawakens the child in us by providing that extraordinary and undifferentiated stimulation—fantastic, scientific, emotional, projected, fearsome, heroic—that for most people is available only in their youth. Educational programs and museum-quality exhibits abound; the detailed furnishings and decor of the various parks are incredibly accomplished and fascinating, if only in a weird, kitsch-culture way; the menu of thrill rides and amusements offered says reams about American pop culture, if you are inclined to muse while standing in line; and the park's undeniable magnetism for tourists of all ages is itself a sociological marvel. At least a dozen languages can be heard not only at EPCOT but all over the World.

The park is increasingly interactive, as the Imagineers would say. The areas where the experience is the most passive in Fjellman's sense are the older ones, the ones connected to the fairy tales and the American-nostalgia settings that were the original basis of the vision: the Magic Kingdom, Cinderella Castle, Frontierland, etc. But much of the later areas, designed not merely for parents but for adults as individuals, are far more sophisticated, especially in their psychological aspects, than those in the older, simpler, more specifically child-amusement days.

"Rides" is an almost laughably inadequate term for these full sensory simulations. You *are* there, in sometimes terrifying ways. When one takes the Body Wars ride in the Wonders of Life Pavilion at EPCOT (which uses entirely convincing physical effects as well as visual cues to induce the sensations of motion, speed, even vertigo) the vast pulsing we are subjected to, momentarily "trapped" in the valve of an artery, taps our deepest ambiguities about the mysteries of the heart itself. We are not only coming as close to real medical wonders as most of us will ever get, but we are momentarily exposed to what a lot of Zen scholars and contemplatives have been after all their lives: rebirth. We are hearing that heartbeat, vibrating to it, in the overwhelming way we did in the womb. It is scary, it is astonishing—and it should be, for any intelligent adult, a prescient reminder of our real humanity.

The theatrically-produced rides at Walt Disney World more usefully answer the emotional needs of children, those in grade school particularly, than mindless roller coasters or "monster rides." The scary parts—

the ghosts and bones and occasional apparent death or animal struggle—are dealt with in an imaginative and often humorous way. (Walt Disney himself, whose true-nature animal films were among his most successful, never shrank from showing real-life violence, although he wasn't so open-minded about sex.)

Yet even when these scary characters are not comic, they're arousing. The transformation of Maleficent, the evil fairy in *Sleeping Beauty,* into a dragon is one of the most chilling and artistically perfect sequences in animation history; the moral, that her destruction by the Prince is a victory of right over might, and good over evil, is made more satisfying by its tension.

But it *is* a victory. At the end of the Disney frights, there is always safety, reward, heroism, redemption. Compare that to the body counts of Freddy's and Jason's endless massacres. Remember, too, that a lot of the characters created or re-created at Disney World are allowed to be imperfect: Indy Jones can be vain and pigheaded; apprentice sorcerer Mickey is lazy and disobedient (and gets bailed out by the stern paternal magician); and so on.

It is certainly true that Walt Disney World lays a veneer of cultural referencing over every aspect of the park, not only in the amusements, but in hotels and dining rooms. But these references have grown steadily broader and more, well, multicultural. It may be the most infuriating ride in history, at least in terms of its theme song, but It's a Small World, created for the 1964 World's Fair, was at least a well-intentioned salute to what we now call the global village. The pavilions of EPCOT's World Showcase are the equal of any world's fair offering, and in at least a few cases arts and traditions that are vanishing in the real world—the delicate and reticent juggler outside the Japan pavilion suggests one—are being conserved in the Disney World.

If it's true that Disney World is sometimes reactive or frankly greedy in its planning and design—imitating major film hits, adding New Orleans– or Key West– or New England–style attractions as those cultures become trendy—it is certainly not alone. In fact, some of those cities are re-creating themselves to attract the same sort of tourist business. If the Disney World resorts are artificial, if a turn-of-the-century wilderness lodge, Cape Cod cottage, Santa Fe adobe, or a luau cove aren't indigenous to central Florida, what does that matter? People shell out huge sums of money not just to stay at Robert Redford's Sundance resort but to buy furniture from its catalogue and decorate their homes with mechanically-weathered cupboards and wrought iron gates. And in truth, these fantasy getaways can be more restorative and probably more informative than vacations to real but, to many people, loud, crowded, smoky, and unintelligible foreign countries.

For several years, park personnel have been leading gardening and cooking "seminars" and behind-the-scenes tours. With the opening of the Disney Institute, the company has provided what may turn out to be the most successful—not merely commercially profitable, but spiritually satisfying—personal retreat many Americans ever experience. For the increasing number of adults who sign up for therapy, New Age seminars, holistic resorts, yoga, or t'ai chi lessons, the chance to tap a long-neglected talent, such as painting or animation or drama, may provide a far more lasting satisfaction. Yes, it is a way, as one Institute guest put it, "to attract a whole segment of the population that wouldn't otherwise have come here," but that doesn't mean it isn't worthwhile. Engagement, not withdrawal, is the secret to fulfillment, and a creative outlet is a truer "antidote to civilization" than any three-day escape to Utopia.

Even more importantly, the Disney "universe," far from offering only escape from the so-called real world, offers techniques for solving many of our everyday frustrations. Yes, Walt Disney wanted total control of his Florida kingdom because he was infuriated by the gaudy development that crowded up around his first park in Los Angeles. Yes, the company has used its muscle shamelessly to get advantageous zoning decisions, highway improvements, and tax credits—and not always either tactfully or perhaps straightforwardly. (In the inadvertently telling phrase of Stephen Joseph Rabori, who offered his master's thesis in planning at the University of Tennessee on the park's design in 1993, "Walt Disney World has tested the authority of government" in its drive to reinvent infrastructure and management.)

But Disney's broader concerns about what he saw taking place in Eisenhower-boom California—the increasing pollution, the decrepit housing, the widening social division, the auto-centric transportation planning—led him to develop methods of public transportation, ecologically beneficent plantings, and conflict-free crowd control. His mandate to protect the environment—observed to an extent almost unheard of in its day—led to the park's sophisticated water control and energy-efficiency techniques, and to the establishment of more than 7,500 acres of permanent wilderness preserve and the 11-acre Discovery Island wildlife sanctuary in Bay Lake. In 1992, Disney purchased the 8,500-acre Walker Ranch and turned it over to the Nature Conservancy, a deal that benefitted the company but helped the restoration effort just as much.

If Walt Disney World reminds us of the freedom of violence-free society, all the better. What else is going to drive us to protest violence or help us teach our children consideration? The civility that is so often remarked on—the willingness of people to wait in line, to make allowances for young children, to smile, and to speak politely—may begin as a sort of park "peer pressure," but civility, like anything else, is a matter of reinforcement. Once practiced—once enjoyed—it is more apt to become habitual.

If so many of Disney's film and television characters are used to raise the park's profile among young children and to reinforce the urge to buy Disney-specific souvenirs, that's a commodity trap worth remembering (or at least budgeting for). But what are the alternatives? Every children's show, even *Sesame Street* and *The Muppets,* has marketing tie-ins, and most are far less innocent than T-shirts and stuffed animals. Considering the amount of violence in such shows as *Power Rangers* and *Transformers,* the Teenage Mutant Ninja Turtles—acrobatic tao-boys with Renaissance painters' names and pizza joneses—are a relatively benign addition to Mr. Disney's Neighborhood.

Even in the "hidden" world that Fjellman wants us to keep in mind as evidence of manipulation there are more universal parallels. When I think of the network of utility tunnels under the castle, I remember the catacombs of Rome and the sewers of Paris; I think of the efforts of architects and urban planners to increase the "livability" of real cities by using just the same sort of concealed power lines and service corridors; I think of the body itself, with all its myriad wonders of blood vessels and tendons and muscles; and I view the park as the imagination set free to walk.

All of this is not to say "Pay no attention to the man behind the curtain." Indeed, this book is primarily about the Wizard, and how he chose to offer us that heart (Fantasyland), or that brain (EPCOT), or that nerve (Body Wars). Of course he has a darker side, a corporate agenda. But his real gift has been to keep alive our sense of adventure and, at his best, our sense of wonder. As Dorothy and her friends learned by taking the Yellow Brick Road—an odyssey re-created in The Great Movie Ride at Disney-MGM Studios—the destination is more often within you than without. We're all going to Walt Disney World, it seems, so keep a smile on your face and your hands inside the boat.

IN THE BEGINNING

The Buying of Walt Disney World

*I*t was almost Kismet—Kismet, Florida. But even then, it might not have been big enough for Walt Disney's dream.

Walt Disney World is nearly 30,000 acres, or 48 square miles. That's more than 80 times the size of Monaco. Grace Kelly would have been queen of a larger, and wealthier, kingdom if she'd married Uncle Walt instead of Prince Rainier.

But the vastness of Walt Disney World was no happy accident. Disney had made one mistake building his first kingdom—not building a big enough "moat" around it—and he wasn't about to make it with the second one. "One thing I learned from Disneyland," Walt Disney once groused, "was to control the environment." Almost as soon as Disneyland opened in 1955, motel operators, fast-food franchises, and tacky souvenir shops tried to camp as close to the castle door as possible. The entrance to the Anaheim park is on Harbour Boulevard, and that jerry-built, neon-splattered strip became the company's version of the Alamo: "Never again!"

After watching what happened to the periphery of Disneyland once the get-rich-quick jackals moved in, Walt Disney was determined that the next time he would control the visual horizon in every direction, no matter how much land it took. The illusion, the controlled perspective, would not blur even at the edges. That has remained one of the most remarkable aspects of the park today. Despite its (now) urbanized location, Walt Disney World seems to exist entirely apart from any city, as if the Orlando Airport, with its monorail-like transit system and its immaculate cleanliness, were the first terminal of this new World. Once inside the "perimeter"—and even that sounds like some futuristic containment center—no concrete skyscrapers, no truck exhaust, no billboards, no power lines interrupt the perfect sky.

In fact, with what most of those Anaheim entrepreneurs would have considered an insane waste of buildable space, Disney World has kept huge stretches of the park near the highways as green buffer zones, allowing the eye and the mind to forget the scale and even the shape of the outside world. The first construction you actually reach after leaving Interstate 4 are hotels, but from the fantastic furbelows, columns, and Claus Oldenberg–sized golf tees—and the giant swans, dolphins, and Triton's horns lavished on them —you'd take them for fairy tale sets at the least.

An unblemished vista wasn't the only consideration, of course: Disney wanted to hold enough territory to exercise total control over development in the
practical sense as well. For one thing, in the first
decade that Disneyland was open, the merchants in
the area just outside the park bled off an incredible
amount of the entertainment dollars that would otherwise have been spent inside. By one estimate, the
exploiters made twice the money Disney did. Dealing
with Anaheim's local utilities cost him a fortune as
well: He had to pay for installing power lines a second
time in order to have them buried underground.

So, for Disney, the aesthetics and the economics
went hand in hand. That meant finding a large
enough tract of undeveloped, or at least minimally
developed, land that at the same time would be acces-
sible—under Disney's own terms—to the millions of
people he needed to attract. The site needed to be in
a fairly warm climate so that it could operate year-
round. That eliminated such early suggestions as Nia-
gara Falls, Baltimore, and Washington, D.C. (although
in the mid-'90s the Disney Company embarked on
another preliminary land-buying binge for an Amer-
ican-history park outside Washington before other
wealthy landowners with better-connected lobbyists
blocked it).

Disneyland's success was so great that any number
of cities tried to interest Walt in a joint venture.
Among the more serious contenders were a group of
developers in St. Louis who were looking for a tourist

draw along the Mississippi River front; Disney considered their proposal fairly seriously until beer magnate Adolph Busch stood up at a business dinner and demanded the park sell beer. Not only did that scotch the St. Louis location, Walt Disney prohibited the sale of any alcohol anywhere in Walt Disney World—a prohibition that lasted until the mid-'80s. (Although alcohol is increasingly obvious around other areas of the park, as discussed in "Pleasure World," it is still prohibited in the Magic Kingdom.)

Orlando wasn't even the only part of the state Disney considered. He had traffic surveys and forecasts prepared for the entire region, which began to pinpoint the central "girdle" where the Florida Turnpike links I-4, I-75 (then in the planning stages), and I-10. Although the state had endured a series of building booms and land sale frauds so notorious that the Marx Brothers set their comedy *Coconuts* around it, the middle stretches were still largely undeveloped and could be had relatively cheaply. Disney prospectors seriously evaluated a large tract along the border of Martin and Palm Beach, as well as the Osceola-Orange area.

In fact, Walt even considered coming home—to Kismet, Florida, a then-tiny and now-vanished town in Volusia County where his parents were married. Although Walt himself was not born there (his parents had moved to Chicago after the collapse of the citrus industry, just before the turn of the century), he had family there and had visited several times as a child. (Volusia is also where Ponce de León landed in his search for the Fountain of Youth; he should have tried Orlando.)

But it was the beauty of the area itself—the mixture of pasture, forest, and marsh—that finally sold Walt Disney on his future kingdom. In 1964, when Disney had his pilots swing the corporate Gulfstream over the pine swamps of central Florida, he pointed out a spot about 15 miles south of Orlando where an unfinished expressway (soon to be the Florida Turnpike) was scraping toward Interstate 4. Then Disney caught a glimpse of a little island in the blue of Bay Lake. "Great," he pronounced. "Buy it." (It is now Discovery Island.)

Disney also quickly dispensed with the Harbour Boulevard problem. When at one early meeting his brother Roy, the financial fall guy, objected to buying yet more land, saying, "We already own about 12,500 acres," Walt shot back:

"Two questions: Is the price right? Do we have the money?"

"Yes to both," his brother conceded.

"Okay," Walt said, ending the discussion. "How would you like to own 10,000 acres next to Disneyland right now?"

But even that didn't quite satisfy Walt. "If he could have," one of his key staffers said later, "he would have bought 50,000 acres."

• Florida B.D.: Before Disney World •

Before it was Walt Disney World, central Florida was primarily agricultural, a combination of cattle ranches, orange groves, and cypress swamps filled with alligators, wild hogs, deer, bobcats, heavenly-colored birds, and hellishly avid bugs. It was also notoriously prone to economic boom-and-bust cycles, a history that perhaps added in the '60s to some local skeptics' dread of the Disney invasion.

The Orlando area shook off a little swamp dust in the 1880s, when the first railroad was laid and farmers discovered the commercial potential of the native citrus groves; it bit that dust for the first time only a few years later, when back-to-back freezes at the end of 1894 and the early weeks of 1895 wiped out the crop and killed off most of the trees. (About the same time, Hamilton Disston bought four million acres of the Everglades for two bits an acre, and set about draining them.) Many of the farmers and homesteaders left the area, including Walt Disney's parents.

A second boom, this one based on the real estate business, and even more feverishly inflationary, puffed up Florida after World War I. The combination of affordable automobiles, cheap land, and hospitable climate pushed land prices into the skies. Ponzi-style speculators made small down payments on huge lots and then sold off the land, at even more extravagant prices, to outlanders who mooned over idealized and often completely fictional land brochures. Orlando authorities issued more than $8.5 million worth of building permits in 1925; there were nearly 5,000 realtors, at least so-called, in that city alone. Miami/ Dade County's land fever was running even higher.

But the first shock wave that ran through the New York stock market in 1926 cracked the facade. The National Better Business Bureau began investigating the fraudulent real estate promotions, and a devastating hurricane that killed nearly 400 persons and laid waste to most of Miami and southern Florida knocked the "paradise" vision on its end. Bankruptcies and foreclosures became routine; the city slashed its budget; and the Chamber of Commerce nearly went under.

Things remained fairly quiet until after World War II, when a more genteel, monied group of summer resort hotels opened, catering to the likes of the Astors and Rockefellers. The area's lake and beaches were studded with rent-a-canoe docks and public ballrooms, but it still trailed well behind Miami and the Keys as a vacation spot.

Space technology companies that were moving into the Canaveral neighborhood had fueled a smallish but comfortable regional boom in the late '50s, beginning with Martin-Marietta and its Pershing missiles plant. But they were already beginning to lay off workers. And it was clear from the shrinking crowds that the space program was already losing its novelty. Even the resort havens of Sarasota, Tampa, and Daytona Beach flourished only seasonally. There was already a semi-official retirement industry, but in those days, senior citizens were not considered or courted as consumers. (That particular inspiration of Disney's—to invent a theme park that would not only accommodate older patrons but actively attract them and exploit their relative wealth of leisure time—has been one of his most emulated innovations.) And in the '60s, after all, most trend-trackers were focusing on the New American Youth, not their grandparents.

By 1964, the Orlando area had as its only major tourist draw the former Cape Canaveral, recently and mournfully rechristened the Kennedy Space Center in honor of the president whose assassination seemed to symbolize the sudden choking off of the nation's postwar vitality and assurance. By the time Disney began feeling out the Florida market, Orlando was ripe for yet another round of development.

The "Mystery Buyer"

From the moment they settled on the Orlando area as their preferred site, it was obvious to Disney and his "Compass East" project team that the company's name must be kept quiet as long as possible to prevent land prices inflating out of reach. So real estate and mortgage agents were hired through layers of dummy developers; many smaller transactions were handled in cash; and correspondence was routed through a post office box address in Kansas City. High-ranking executives traveled under pseudonyms; Disney himself favored the name "Bill Davis." Lawyers representing such dummy firms as Florida Ranch Lands, Latin American Development and Management Corp., and the original Reedy Creek Ranch Corp. began combing through land records, looking for large parcels and potentially willing sellers.

The first crucial contact that Disney representatives made, however, was with Billy Dial, then president of the First National Bank at Orlando. It was to be the making of both Disney World, which financed its construction through Dial and his alliance, and of the institution, now SunTrust, one of the dominant banks in the region and the only one that operates— with its tellers in turn-of-the-century Main Street costume—within Disney World itself.

The second crucial interview was, at Dial's urging and to Disney's surprise, with then-publisher Martin Andersen of the *Orlando Sentinel.* (Dial had previously been an attorney for the *Sentinel* and remained a close friend and confidant of Andersen.) Disney attorneys told Andersen that rumors of the move had already surfaced in California, and they were concerned it might spread to Florida before they were ready to announce. Amazingly, Andersen agreed to delay publicizing or publicly speculating on the mysterious purchasers until most of the essential lots were in hand. In fact, he even agreed not to disclose the Disney connection to his own reporting staff, and ordered his key editorial staffers to do the same.

In many cases, the land booms of earlier decades

paid belated dividends to the Disney team. Much of the lakefront land had been sold by mail order catalogue in 1913, and Disney's dummy companies were often able to take advantage of the casual ignorance of landowners who had never seen their holdings, had inherited them or had them transferred through business swaps, or who had found themselves in possession of a swamp or forest they could never afford to develop. Disney's plan was to buy up smaller parcels from absentee owners and take options on crucial major tracts.

The first really large purchase was from the legendary Florida state senator Irlo "Bud" Bronson in late 1964; he sold 8,380 acres of base scrub and swamp for a little over $100 an acre—and on a handshake deal at that. (Later, when the identity of the purchaser was made public, Bronson's son asked him about backing out, but the senator said he had to stick by his word.) Not until May, 1965, when that deed of sale and one other were recorded by the Osceola County Clerk, did the first *Sentinel* story appear—with a pointed warning against "speculation" as to the identity of the mystery client.

Most of the early rumors, in fact, centered on the space industry and aviation companies: Lockheed, Howard Hughes, McDonnell and Douglas, Republic, PhilCo. At least one television announcer fell victim to jokesters who sent him an urgent telegram that said the mystery buyer was Ford Motor Company. He interrupted the telecast to read it on camera. There were great congratulations on-screen, until a few minutes later, when the follow-up telegram arrived: "They want to pasture out their Mustangs."

More suspects were tossed about: Great Lakes Steel, Boeing, General Electric, Chrysler, Volkswagen, even the Rockefeller family. The *Sentinel* itself, in an astonishing bit of prevarication that it spent years having to live down, published a story that referred to the notion that "the land is being purchased for a second East Coast Disneyland attraction." But they announced that "little credence is being given this in view of the fact that Walt Disney himself, in a recent statement to the *Orlando Sentinel* while on a visit to Cape Kennedy, said he was spending $50 million to expand his California attraction and . . . had his hands full."

Only three days later, however, the paper admitted in an editorial that it had not only promised not to reveal the company's identity, but had helped the company buy a 35-acre tract "they wanted and needed." By the end of May, the rival *Evening Star* had uncovered a $5 million package of 47 purchases made through an Orlando brokerage firm, totaling 27,250 acres. In effect, Disney had purchased his kingdom for less than $200 an acre; within months, would-be carpetbaggers were paying around $40,000 an acre, with prime tracks going for five or six times that.

Andersen managed to keep the Disney name a close secret for five months, until one of his more dogged reporters, Emily Bavar, editor of the *Sentinel*'s Sunday magazine, caught Walt Disney himself off guard during an interview in California. By then, rather than categorically deny the question, Disney merely replied, "I'd rather not say," which, as any reporter knows, is an affirmative response. Bavar immediately wrote that the mystery investor was Disney.

Bavar's story was intentionally underplayed by the *Sentinel*'s management, but even so, it was clear the time had come to let the Mouse out of the bag. On October 24, 1965, the *Sentinel* ran another editorial, this one exuberantly pro-Disney and pro-development. The adjectives used included "fantastic," "fabulous," and "prosperous." It promised that Orlando would become "the greatest tourist city in the world," and that the benefits would be universal. "The magic of this modern Merlin will touch us all here in this promised land of prosperity." That the details of this "fabulous" plan were still entirely secret didn't seem to bother anyone at the time. The next day, then-Governor Haydon Burns, who had also been in on the secret from the beginning, made the formal announcement at the convention of the Florida municipal league in Miami.

A Mouse in the House (of Representatives)

Over the next year, the future World was largely a matter of political feint and parry. Disney, still committed to the rule of total control, blanketed the state legislature with lobbyists and consultants polishing

friendly statutes, particularly on the subject of highway improvements. In the beginning, Florida voters
turned down a road bond issue worth $300 million
that would have paid for many of those improvements. Although it was not a particularly anti-Disney
vote, just an anti-tax one, it apparently surprised the
self-absorbed Disney corporation—and sounded the
first warning to state residents that they wouldn't be
getting this tourist industry treasure trove without
investing a few coins themselves.

But on December 15, 1966, Walt Disney, who had
been battling lung cancer, died of complications.
Despite the corporation's assurances, Disney's death
threatened to break the political spell. So in February,
1967, the Disney organization gathered its forces in
nearby Winter Haven for a final strategic push. Before
an audience including Florida Governor Claude Kirk
and his cabinet, the state legislature, business leaders,
and media, the corporation laid out a plan including
a Disneyland-like amusement park, theme motels,
sports and recreational areas "which will take advantage of and preserve the natural beauty of the area," an
industrial park for state-of-the-art technologies, and
a jetport to handle private charters and "executive
planes."

It also, for the first time, mentioned the "Experimental Prototype Community of Tomorrow, planned
for 20,000 permanent residents." That prototype,
EPCOT, was the main subject of a prerecorded 25-
minute video starring Walt Disney himself—a sort of

sales pitch from beyond the grave. While most of us are more familiar with Walt from the vault than the man himself, thanks to those TV clips and even the bits of video still used at the parks, on that day, less than two months after his death, his obvious sincerity and conviction made a strong impression on his official audience.

Disney called EPCOT "the heart of everything we'll be doing."

EPCOT, he went on, "will never be completed, but will always be introducing and testing and demonstrating new materials and systems. . . . We're convinced [that] the need is not just for curing old ills of old cities, or even just building a whole new shiny city. We think the need is for starting from scratch on virgin land like this, and building a special kind of community. . . . Everything in EPCOT will be dedicated to the happiness of the people who live here and work here [as well as] those who come here from all around the world."

That influx of tourists, historians have pointed out, was the bait. Then came the hook: "We must have the flexibility . . . to work in cooperation with American industry, and to make decisions based on standards of performance. If we have this kind of freedom, I'm confident we can create a world showcase for American free enterprise that will bring new industry to the state of Florida from all over the country." In other words, don't tangle us up with red tape, and we'll make enough money for both of us.

Governor Kirk agreed, saying the state would gar-
ner $4 billion in tourist income in the first 10 years
alone, plus additional revenues from new construction
and permanent service jobs. (He was too conservative:
In 1981, an *Orlando Sentinel* business reporter said
that Disney World had "stimulated economic activity
in its first year to a degree originally forecast more
than 10 years in the future.") Kirk was among early
boosters who helped Disney put a pretty face on its
iron control by supporting its proposal to combine its
holdings into the Reedy Creek Improvement District—to become its own government. On May 12,
1967, Governor Kirk signed the bills establishing the
Reedy Creek entity; he called "the magic moment that
Walt and Roy Disney decided to make Florida their
second home a landmark in Florida history equaled
only by the arrival of Ponce de León and the opening
of the railroad to Palm Beach." That same day, the
state road board voted to divert $5 million over the
next five years to start on highway improvements near
the park.

At the local level, however, politicians felt a little
less enthusiastic about the sort of legislative flexibility the company was talking about. In effect, Disney
was going over the heads of both Osceola County and
Orange County to zone, develop, tax, and administer
itself. One big savings to Disney, for example, was in
impact fees that one local commissioner estimated
would have cost more than $18 million per hotel (in
1971 dollars, at that).

By 1967, *Orlando Sentinel* publisher Andersen had either had time to think things through in more depth, or at least to be embarrassed into rediscovering his journalistic objectivity. The *Sentinel* began to run stories and editorials questioning whether the state was really ready to absorb such a huge and revolutionary project, and speculating on the potential drawbacks of granting Reedy Creek such autonomy.

They had a point. In the early years especially, Walt Disney World had a pretty high-handed attitude toward the state and local governments. Instead of expanding a twisting, old, two-lane delivery road that was supposedly the employee entrance, Disney launched a public relations campaign calling the road dangerous and finally forcing the state to have it rebuilt. One Orange County commission estimated that by the time the park opened in 1971, Walt Disney World had cost the county $12–14 million in funds that had to be withdrawn from previously okayed improvements. A later flap over state bonds that Reedy Creek obtained for development was even more bitter: The bonds had certainly been legally obtained, but many felt Disney was not living up to the spirit of the agreement—especially since several other jurisdictions had planned to use the bonds for low-cost housing and other social welfare programs.

Disney's presence did make land many times more valuable than it had been, but that also meant painful increases in tax assessments for residents. Many longtime ranchers had to sell off their lands because of the inflated taxes. Disney itself, the beneficiary of so many special exceptions, fought a very long battle against the Orange County assessor to get its taxes lowered, giving it a reputation for corporate egocentricity that it has never quite shaken.

Nevertheless, Disney has unquestionably been an economic boon to Orlando, turning the entire region into a prime investment market and one of the top tourist destinations anywhere. Its property taxes add scores of millions to local budgets every year. Every time a new resort or theme park is built and opens, thousands of new construction and permanent jobs are added to the regional economy.

And over the last several years, the Disney Company has worked hard to improve its community image, handing out grants (with plenty of publicity) and establishing minority programs, albeit under some pressure. To soothe concerns over previous animal-rights debacles (see "Animal, Vegetable, or Mineral?"), Disney has set up an advisory board of wildlife and conservation experts to oversee its plans for a wild animal park. Its new Celebration community (see "The Mouse that Scored") is expected to produce another $42 million a year in property taxes, more than doubling Osceola County's revenues.

"They're actually much better now," as one businessman put it. "They used to say, 'Hey, we made you what you are.' Now it's, 'Remember, we have to live here, too.'"

The manager of a nearby hotel franchise, interviewed by the *Sentinel* about Disney's building of budget hotels, took it in stride. "This is a capitalistic society. I look at it this way: If Disney wasn't here, we'd all be sitting in orange groves."

The Vision Comes into Focus

When Walt Disney first contemplated his Eastern kingdom, he recognized that even if he succeeded in getting the state to take a hands-off approach to the project, it would be best to get the construction physically underway as quickly and smoothly as possible— demonstrating that his company was as cutting-edge as promised, while effectively squelching any protests before they had time to arise. To do that, he hired a pair of engineering experts with experience in the snap-to world of the armed services: former Army Corps of Engineers Major General William E. "Joe" Potter, who had been Robert Moses' second-in-command at the New York World's Fair; and retired Admiral Joe Fowler, who had also headed up the construction at Disneyland. Fowler's presence tipped off at least one Orlando real estate broker, who was driving one of the dummy-company attorneys around town. The driver heard his passenger address a companion as "Admiral," and that night spotted a photograph in a *National Geographic* story profiling Fowler as "the man who built Disneyland." Fortunately for Disney, he kept his sleuthing to himself.

As Walt Disney began to expand his vision of the

site to include not only the park itself but a sort of science-and-tech Utopia, he gave himself a crash course in planning, technology, and what would now be considered market research. He had Potter send letters to 500 foundations and research centers and set up 100 personal visits. He toured shopping malls and pedestrian centers and read the latest reports on urban planning and environmental advances. Battling cancer, he researched cryonics, the freezing of human bodies for future defrosting and, presumably, healing. This fascination led to one of Walt Disney World's most resilient myths: Disney himself is lying in icy state in an upper room of Cinderella Castle.

By the time Walt died, he had pretty much set the tone for the park's wide-ranging interests: the solar and even nuclear-power experiments, sustainable agriculture, and robotic and synthetic "life."

In 1968, the Disney Company raised $90 million in bond sales for construction and took out a line of credit worth $50 million from a consortium of banks (although, since the company stock kept going up, virtually all its debts were paid before the park was complete).

The company forged an agreement with the labor unions in 1969 that ensured a strike-free project in return for swift good-faith negotiation of disagreements. There was another trade-off involved: Disney proposed to pay lower wages than some other Florida developers, but it did promise to hire through the unions. That, in the long run, was more important to the AFL-CIO. Opening day was set for October 1, 1971.

But in 1970, the California-based construction firm said the park would not, could not, be ready on time. But the farm, so to speak, had all been mortgaged; the show had to go on. So the construction firm was fired, and a little financial sleight of hand allowed Disney to lease the equipment and take on the job itself. It came close to failing: Dick Nunis, then director of operations and later president of the park, told the *Sentinel* that in the last weeks, he suddenly realized no worker was expecting to come in on Labor Day. Gritting his teeth, Nunis was inspired to invite the workers and their families to picnic at the unfinished park, and they worked with renewed dedication for the rest of the time.

About two months before the opening, *Life* magazine sent out a photographer to take a picture. Despite the looming deadlines, Disney executives decided to take the fullest advantage of the publicity. They called up the entire cast of characters in full costume and makeup, from the Mouse to the Seven Dwarfs, and posed them in front of Cinderella's Castle. All the musicians, greeters, ride attendants, cooks, and even the street sweepers, were lined up behind them. The *Life* photographer, in the style of those days, set up spots and extra lighting to excise any potential shadows (it was full sunlight and pushing 100°, according to some reports), and then, hoisted overhead in a cherry picker, he began to take test shots and light measurements. Hours passed. Various cast members fainted and had to be replaced by newly costumed and made-up characters, and Nunis fumed and paced. Finally, photographer Yale Joel took one perfect frame—and it is still one of the best covers that ever graced that photo-phile magazine. It ran on October 15, 1971.

Ten days or so before the opening, a group of national tourist executives and legislators came for a tour; they were "flabbergasted," one remembers, but they did wonder where all the trees were. Requests for interviews, free tickets, and charity appearances came so fast and furious that one secretary finally screamed, "I can't take it anymore!" and tossed her telephone right through the wall.

One *Sentinel* reporter sneaked into the *Hall of Presidents* on the last day, claiming to be part of the work crew. When he finished his shift, he walked out toward what had been a flat field— it had turned into a grassy hill.

The night before, or rather the morning of, the grand opening, the head of publicity finally went home at 1 A.M.; the press room had no telephones and no typewriters, no floor coverings, no wallpaper, and only a few light bulbs. But when he returned at 5 A.M., the press center was ready.

On opening day everyone involved in the project was frantic. At 10 A.M. another intrepid reporter discovered, the paint on the walls of the ice cream parlor was still wet. National predictions that the park would draw huge crowds—or fail if it didn't—had Disney employees dizzy and dreading disaster.

The park neither drew a huge crowd, nor failed. That first morning, despite a swarm of traffic helicopters and state troopers, only about 9,000 paying guests showed up, met by 5,000 frantically smiling employees. Some Disney veterans claim that the "soft opening" was intentional, that they had picked a slow month and a slow day, Friday, so that the cast would have time to work out the kinks. But most kept their fingers crossed for the holidays, and sure enough, on the Friday after Thanksgiving, more than 200,000 would-be guests were stalled in traffic on I-4. The park had to close the gate by mid-morning.

It was the beginning of the World.

• Walt's World A.D.: After Disney •

In the tense months of 1967 right after Walt Disney's death, when the kingdom was suddenly without its chief visionary, the company's key executives agonized over whether it would be possible to build the park without him. Roy Disney, who had been planning to retire, finally said, "Can we do it without Walt? We don't know—but let's try. And remember, we're not going to spend one penny over $125 million." The Magic Kingdom would wind up costing more than three times that.

But what the park earned blew away any predictions, too. In its first year, according to corporate reports, the park made nearly a 22-million-dollar profit, which was just about what the financially acute Roy Disney had predicted. The next year, profits rose to $40 million; and by 1980, they had doubled again. In its first ten years, Walt Disney World made nearly $2.5 billion. By 1987, it had one-year profits of $450 million, and makes more than twice that now.

Attendance figures to Walt Disney World also went way beyond the Disney brothers' expectations. Forty million people visited Walt Disney World in its first four years, and a total of 125 million visited in its first ten years. But that was just the beginning: attendance was up to 25 million a year in 1987, 26 million in 1988, and 32 million in 1990.

In the early '90s, when the Persian Gulf War pushed gasoline prices up and new entertainment meccas beckoned in Branson, Missouri, and Myrtle Beach, Disney World attendance stalled and even declined a bit. By 1994, attendance was down 5%— a drop most Orlando-area executives and analysts blamed on new chairman Michael Eisner's decision to hike ticket prices. However, toward the end of that year, Eisner announced a new marketing strategy with a 116-million-dollar budget, and Disney opened its first budget hotels, the All-Star Sports and All-Star Music resorts. By 1995, attendance at Walt Disney World was back up an estimated 15% to 34 million visitors. Over the 1995–1996 holiday season, when most companies were reporting low consumer interest and shrinking profits, the Walt Disney Co. posted new highs in theme-park attendance and souvenir sales, with profits up 14%.

THE WORLD ACCORDING TO WALT

Walt Disney's America

*W*hen Walt Disney talked about "children of all ages," he meant it literally. Walt Disney dreamed of building a place to take his own children that would bear no resemblance to the traditional beer gardens and midways, a place of innocent delight and inspiration. And what an adult holds dearest, what he hopes to convey to his children, is usually the things he himself cherished when young. The child is not only father to the man, but to his children. So before entering Walt's ultimate "World," it's worth stopping to remember the world he grew up in: the world and especially the America that inspired him, and the one he tried to re-create in his parks.

The quarter-century before and the first decade after Walt Disney's birth spanned, fittingly, one of the greatest eras of "imagineering" in history. It was the heyday of the great expositions and the early World's Fairs: the Philadelphia Exhibition of 1876, the Columbian Exposition of 1893 in Chicago, the Paris Expositions of 1889 and 1900. George Eastman's photographic paper replaced painfully slow glass plates, followed in increasingly short order by celluloid film, the box camera, and the motion picture cameras. Freeze-frame photography revealed the wonders of the running man, and stop-film cameras the potential of animation. H. G. Wells ruminated on time travel and Einstein on relativity. The first electric submarines, and then the first diesel-powered ones, carried deep-sea explorers into that other great unknown.

It was, especially in America, the age of the legendary inventors: Alexander Graham Bell, the Wright brothers, Thomas Edison. Electrification wrought one of the greatest revolutions: the extension of daylight. The assembly line produced commodities, and they eventually produced the consumer. The first plastics were created, and the first synthetics. Steel mills were transforming what had been an agricultural-mercantile society into the beginnings of an industrial one—and at least in that one period, great fortunes did trickle down: Andrew Carnegie's money built a great public opera house and opened libraries all over the country.

It was the era of the transatlantic cruise, the Great Tour, and the travelogue. It was the era of personal freedom as well, of motorized bicycles, pneumatic tires, and internal combustion, and the names Diesel, Benz, Ford, and Rolls-Royce.

It was a time when we took for granted the great rivers and the Mississippi paddle wheelers and leaped over them to the captured frontier. It was the age of the Yukon gold rush, the land booms, and the homestead acts; the age of Chief Joseph, Geronimo, and the Indian reservations. It was the era of gunslingers and desperados whose exploits were exaggerated by penny-dreadful books of "frontier justice" and Judge Roy Bean. The buffalo herds were replaced by the cattle drives, and Buffalo Bill took his "Wild West Show" to Europe.

It was the beginning of the communications era: Alexander Graham Bell put the private citizen "on line" for the first time, followed by the telegraph system and radio transmission. It was the era of the shrinking globe, of the new steam engines and the great railroads that inexorably marked off America, Siberia, Canada, the "Orient," and the "Levant." It was the era of the explorer-hero, of Richard Burton, Livingston and Stanley, Amundsen and Peary. In the years before Disney's birth, Heinrich Schliemann uncovered Troy and Mycenae; when Disney was only 20, Howard Carter broke through into the Tomb of Tut. Gauguin went to Tahiti and the U.S. Army to Hawaii. It was the age of Suez and the Panama Canal, of *The Arabian Knights, Tarzan of the Apes,* and *King Solomon's Mines.*

It was the age of vast and even world-wide epidemics: typhoid (which struck Disney's father), tuberculosis (which brother Roy contracted), and the virulent influenza of 1918, which nearly killed Walt himself. But it was also the era of radioactivity and antiseptics, the control of yellow fever, and the application of X-rays.

It was a time that confused patriotism and nativism, the era of essential immigrant labor and reactionary anti-immigrant riots. It was a time of international violence, of assassinations and nationalist uprisings and anarchists. The Spanish-American War was engineered by newspaper tycoon and would-be kingmaker William Randolph Hearst. But it was also the era of Wilson's League of Nations, the first serious one-world view articulated in this country, and of the dedication of the Statue of Liberty.

It was the age of the first comic strips, and of the first newsreels. It was a golden age for children's literature: *Wind in the Willows* and *Peter Pan, The Jungle Book* and *Just-So Stories, Alice in Wonderland* and *Uncle Remus, Tom Sawyer* and *Treasure Island,* and *Kidnapped* and Howard Pyle's rousing versions of *Robin Hood* and *King Arthur*—stories Disney turned to when he began to make films. Tchaikovsky's *Nutcracker* and *Sleeping Beauty* were instantly classics, and he remembered them, too.

All these images, all these national obsessions, romances, and heroes, and in particular the explorers and inventors—everything except the plagues and the wars—reappear in the part of Walt's amusement park that was closest to his own vision: the Magic Kingdom. The symbols of various other countries in It's a

Small World, which foreshadow many of the icons at the World Showcase, are straight out of those early newsreels: the Eiffel Tower, the Sphinx, the Acropolis, the Taj Mahal, Big Ben. Walt himself was a talented inventor (it was his multi-plane camera that made convincing three-dimensional animation possible), and like his idols, he used several World's Fairs, starting with the 1939 New York fair, as stages to unveil his technological innovations. Like Carnegie, he sincerely believed that culture should be made available to the masses (a concept that resulted in the kitsch classic *Fantasia*). Like Eadweard Muybridge and George Eastman, he pushed camera technology forward; like Benz and Bell, he dreamed of impulsive travel and instantaneous communication. These same images pop up again and again in the later attractions as well, although, as we'll see, the corporate offspring of Disney had slightly less romanticized views.

• Walt's Own Early History •

Walter Elias Disney was born almost with the 20th century, in 1901. He was the fourth and youngest son of a willing but unlucky man who repeatedly labored to save his own money, spent it on private ventures— a citrus grove in Florida, a cattle farm in Missouri (where Walt was born), a jelly factory in Chicago— and in between, when they failed, took on carpentry or small construction jobs. As a boy, Walt Disney knew the unforgiving face of the Midwest as well as its prodigious energies; Walt often recalled having struggled through terrifying pre-dawn blizzards, delivering newspapers in Kansas City—the sort of schoolboy nightmare people usually tell whoppers about. He was not a quick student anyway, and the added strain of farm chores and getting up at 3 A.M. made him even less successful.

His father was a strict taskmaster who believed his sons' duty was to add to the family fortune, whether they worked at home or outside. When Walt was only six, his two oldest brothers retaliated by getting what they considered their fair share of the family bank account (and a little more) and leaving home. That left only Walt and Roy, and all the money from their newspaper routes and any summer jobs had to be turned over. Walt had to sneak an extra bundle of papers to sell in order to buy even penny candy behind his father's back. By the time he was a teenager, the farm had gone broke again and the family had moved to Chicago. Walt had discovered night classes at the Chicago Art Institute, where he drew the cartoons for the school paper, and he was in a hurry to escape.

Walt had spent one summer selling papers and peanuts on the Santa Fe Railroad, and though he was a spectacular commercial failure—he let himself be shortchanged and cheated with apparent frequency— he was crazy about the trains themselves, and more than a little vain of his shiny-buttoned uniform. In 1918, stretching his age a little, he enlisted in the ambulance corps and headed for Europe. But having arrived after the Armistice was signed, he went to France, where he made a scant living cartooning and painting GI posters and fake German souvenirs and decorations for the victorious American grunts.

When Walt returned, he tried to get a job with his old employer, the *Kansas City Star,* as a cartoonist. They wouldn't hire him as a truck driver. He and his friend Ub Iwerks finally did get jobs with an advertising agency, and in 1920 Walt persuaded a local cinema owner to buy his early animation efforts (short commentaries and timely items called "Laugh-O-Grams") to run as fillers. Like his father, Walt quickly sank all his money into an animation studio of his own; like his father, he quickly went broke. At age 21, bearing a half-finished animated feature called, interestingly, *Alice's Wonderland,* he and Iwerks struck out for California, hoping to find work in one of the commercial studios there. Shortly thereafter he persuaded banker brother Roy to come in with them.

Walt didn't have to wait long for his commercial breakthrough, or so it seemed. Still in his mid-20s, he hit on the character of an earnest and perhaps slightly Goofy rabbit with long floppy ears named Oswald, whose animated adventures were distributed along with films from Universal Pictures by a theater magnate named Charles Mintz. By 1928 there were Oswald candy bars and souvenirs, and Disney, who was a better idea man than draftsman, had hired a studio of animators to help him with the supply. But this first success as a professional animator also led to his first hard lesson in autonomy: When Disney went to ask for more money, he discovered that Universal had, in the fine print, obtained the rights to Oswald—and that, preparing for this moment, Mintz had hired away all but one of Disney's animators, Iwerks himself.

Walt didn't tell Roy that they were broke again immediately, but on the train home to California, the legend goes, he began doodling circles and sticks, and out of that came the Mouse (although, the early Mickey wasn't nearly so spherical as the later version; over time, he just "O"ed). One of the most famous bits of Mickey trivia is that Walt originally considered naming him Mortimer, but thankfully, his wife Lillian demurred.

It was Lucky Lindbergh who literally got Mickey off the ground. Mickey's first film, laid out in 1929, portrayed him as a daredevil pilot in *Plane Crazy*, but *Steamboat Willie*—featuring Mickey at the helm of a great Mississippi paddle wheeler a la Mark Twain, and with Walt's own voice squeaking on the sound track—was released first, and so became Mickey's official debut. *Steamboat Willie* still runs at the Main Street moviehouse in the Magic Kingdom.

It surprises people now to discover that few of Disney's features were immediate commercial successes. *Snow White and the Seven Dwarfs* earned him a bank loan in 1939 by winning a special Academy Award; the next year, *Pinocchio*'s poor reviews cut off his credit. *Fantasia*—Disney's 1940 attempt to wed pop

(Mickey Mouse and *The Nutcracker Suite*) with high culture (*The Firebird* and Leopold Stokowski)—was a colossal flop the first time out, although it is a cult classic today. Starting with shorts in the late '40s, the real-life nature films such as *The Living Desert* (1953) became almost as famous in Disney productions as the Mickey Mouse cartoons, but they were emergency money-makers at the time; the studio might well have gone under otherwise. After Disneyland opened in 1955, however, there was little problem.

The one thing Walt never did after Oswald was to sell or surrender the rights to any film or market tie-in—not even to brother Roy, the company finance man, who stopped speaking to his brother for ten years over the issue of merchandising royalties. But it did mean keeping his own company safe from raiders. That early lesson in the value of total creative and marketing control became the guiding precept behind the making of Walt Disney World.

Walt's Moment in Time

Walt Disney had a dream, but he also had a lucky draw, historically speaking. What he wanted to create might not have been possible, at least not in the form he envisioned, at any other moment in American history.

The first concept parks in this country appeared about the middle of the 19th century, and the most famous, like Coney Island's Luna Park, flourished toward the turn of the century and into Walt's early years. They reflected major changes in American society, most importantly the appearance for the first time of a mass paying audience—a middle class with money and time to spare, and the social drive to indulge both—and the widespread installation of electricity. It was the fantastic possibilities of the lighted midway and the heightened thrills of electrically powered roller coasters that reinvigorated the amusement park. (Although the effects are "boosted" by more up-to-date techniques, it still comes down to flash and splash.)

In the late '40s, when he began to contemplate creating a vacation park, Walt Disney had similar social currents to ride. The wartime and post-war economy had produced a national boom (especially for the new middle class). Americans were beginning to live longer, so there were more grandparents and extended families. The creation of the interstate highway system made attracting tourists from great distances feasible, even—in the early era of driving and family vacations—an exciting prospect. And the development of air conditioning made it as attractive to vacation inside a park setting as at the seaside or in the mountains.

On top of that, Disney himself had the most enticing product of all: escapism. His animated characters were already American institutions. New money, new methods, and what seemed to be unlimited resources: America was a market just waiting to be exploited.

But Walt himself didn't think of it as exploitation.

He was a serious disciple of the American Dream, and he had in mind to act as the living proof. Mickey represented an honest product (this time, one Walt was going to hold on to), a pure spirit and a cheerful heart, and a sort of staggeringly simple pleasure in the exercise of the imagination. "When You Wish Upon a Star" might have been written as the Disney Bill of Rights: "Anything your heart desires will come to you." *That* was the America Walt Disney desired to re-create for his children. So when he designed the Magic Kingdom, Disney looked away from the present and its ambiguities toward the idealized past and the even more ideal future.

There's a famous bit of dialogue in Lewis Carroll's *Alice through the Looking-Glass:*

> *The rule is, "Jam tomorrow and jam yesterday—
>   but never jam to-day."*
> *"It must come sometimes to 'jam to-day'," Alice
>   objected.*
> *"No, it can't," said the Queen. "It's jam every
>   other day: to-day isn't any other day, you
>   know."*
> *"I don't understand you," said Alice. "It's dread-
>   fully confusing!"*
> *"That's the effect of living backwards," the Queen
>   said kindly: "it always makes one a little giddy
>   first—"*
> *"Living backwards!" Alice repeated in great aston-
>   ishment. "I never heard of such a thing!"*

"—but there's one great advantage in it, that one's memory works both ways."

Walt Disney looked into the future and back to the past, but he almost never seemed to find himself in the present. Most of the early attractions recalled, with an exaggerated nostalgia, the brighter eras and the heroes and romances of his childhood: the great explorers, the Wild West, the patriot fathers, the Industrial Revolution, the children's stories.

He especially loved the Victorian Era, calling it America's "innocent years." The Missouri of his childhood was theoretically the inspiration for Main Street, U.S.A., though only in its halcyon summer-vacation moments and stripped of any dismal memories: no blizzards, no doctor's office, and no school-house. Almost no one has a dismal experience in Walt Disney's America, as a matter of fact, at least not that Walt noticed. (Disney World's white-male attitude toward history remains one of its weaker points, as discussed in "America's Adventures in Wonderland: The Disney Version of History.")

Almost every one of Walt Disney World's hotels and resort areas looks backward to some idealized past: Atlantic City between the wars, Florida during the first resort boom, wilderness America in its un-developed sanctity, Gauguin's Polynesia, Crystal Palace Victoriana, the buccaneering Caribbean, even plantation-era Louisiana.

And it's just as well, because the odd thing is, like

jam tomorrow, the "future" never actually arrives. The few futuristic attractions in Disney's original Tomorrowland were forward-looking only in the most romantic and simple fashion—that is, they were gussied-up versions of the past, just as *The Jetsons* was a re-costumed imitation of *The Flintstones*. (In fact, check out the space-cadet uniforms on the line monitors at the *Extra-TERROR-estrial Alien Encounter*; they're straight out of *Flash Gordon*.) The moon rides and technological predictions were borrowed from nineteenth-century visionaries such as Jules Verne and H. G. Wells and even Edgar Allan Poe. The Horizons ride at EPCOT acknowledges this, looking "back at tomorrow" by saluting just those early predictions.

Even the renovated Tomorrowland attractions are 99% past and 1% promise, from Spaceship Earth to the new *Timekeeper* attraction. *Timekeeper* even uses Verne and Wells as characters. The World of Motion exhibit at Future World at EPCOT, which didn't get much further into the future than moving sidewalks, is being replaced by a thrill ride that doesn't even pretend to get out of the '90s: It's a harrowing variation on seat-belt safety hosted by TV's most beloved fall guys, the crash-test dummies.

The Tomorrowland at Disneyland in California is also under renovation, for the third time in its 40 years. When the Imagineers went to Disney CEO Michael Eisner seeking guidance, he reportedly said to them, "How do you create the future when the future looks like Montana?" What he meant was that those

very high-tech people movers and plastic furnishings
that in Walt Disney's time spelled progress, now seem
harsh and impersonal. Eisner believes more and more
Americans want to join the back-to-simplicity movement, heading away from the techno-heavy urban
centers that were Tomorrowland's pretext—and his
conviction is the reason that Disney's first residential
development, Celebration, is being built not as a technological showplace but as a model small town, a true
"community."

At bottom, this future-past is a built-in paradox:
Walt Disney World is full of rousing speeches about
how much better technology is going to make our
lives, and yet, by definition, the computers, vehicles,
and imaging techniques we are seeing already exist.
Certain transportation systems—space travel certainly—are still beyond us. But the concept is old—
there is little new thinking on display. Perhaps this
difficulty is one reason the Eisner-era Disney Co. has
moved away from futuristic predictions and into
futuristic effects, like those at Disney-MGM Studios
and *Alien Encounter,* or back to the equally mysterious
but less rapidly evolving past, like the dinosaur world
under construction (see "The Animal Kingdom"), or
just the day-to-day escapism of sports and self-
fulfillment (see "Pleasure World"). When the new
Disneyland Tomorrowland opens in 1998, it will
focus more on the *process* of creating the future than
any results.

The one truly progressive concept Walt Disney

cherished was EPCOT, his new city of Tomorrow, and even it borrowed heavily—though he would have hated to hear it—from turn-of-the-century philosophy. In any case, EPCOT, the gift Walt Disney envisioned as his legacy to future generations, was transformed by his corporate successors into just another huge pseudo-historic shopping mall, a permanent World's Fair or Exposition, before it ever broke ground. Maybe that's appropriate: Utopia yesterday, Utopia tomorrow, but never Utopia today.

THE MOUSE THAT SCORED

The Michael Eisner Era

*I*t's tempting for those who grew up with the "old" Disney, the animated classics and the clean-cut Mouseketeers, to think of Michael Eisner as the "anti-Walt"—a guy with a corporate outlook instead of a creative one, a schemer rather than a dreamer. And it's true that Eisner has an enormously canny sense of the public appetite and how to feed it.

But in fact, the two have more in common than traditionalists would like to admit. (After all, Walt Disney was no slouch when it came to forging an audience and spinning off side projects.) It was Disney who insisted on buying so much Florida land that it would take generations of development to fill it; it was Eisner who launched the theme parks, resorts, professional sports franchises, and even residential communities to fill it. It was Disney who conceived of the all-ages attraction, and Eisner who understood how to exploit each segment of the expanding audience.

It was Disney who believed so fervently that turn-of-the-century America was the ideal home that he ordered a Main Street in every park he designed, even in Europe and Japan; it was Eisner who said, in connection with the ill-fated American history park in Virginia, that America "is the best of all possible places, [the] place that you are happy you are living in—and if you are not living there, you would love to be part of the American experience."

In some ways, Eisner forms the perfect complement to Disney, the yin to the yang: Disney came from the nation's heartland with more pencil lead than money and built a World—really a universe—of fantastic imagination and frontier-busting technology. Michael Eisner, who came from a world of wealth and cosmopolitan learning, revitalized the Disney Company by returning it to its filmmaking roots. And it is Eisner who is finally building the "community of tomorrow," the town called Celebration, not as a cool futuristic EPCOT, but as a real-life, neighborly minded Main Street, U.S.A.

"Call Me Michael"

One of the heavily promoted aspects of Disney corporate philosophy is that everybody, from the top to the bottom, is on a first-name basis. "He said, 'Call me Michael,'" a still somewhat awed employee said some months after meeting CEO Eisner. Although he's now in his mid-50s, "Mr. Eisner" would seem a little stiff for a guy who is 6'3" with a nose frequently compared to Howdy Doody's and a sheepish little bald spot in the middle of his rumpled hair. (*Washington Post* reporter William Powers once described him as "the man with the Tom Sawyer face and the sandpaper voice.")

Besides, this is the guy who invented *Happy Days* while stranded by a snowstorm in the Newark, NJ, airport and who helped produce such box-office smashes for Paramount as *Saturday Night Fever*, *Raiders of the Lost Ark, Grease, Ordinary People, Star Trek, An Officer and a Gentleman, Flashdance, Friday the 13th, 48 Hrs.,* and *Beverly Hills Cop.* He's the guy who had such faith in one childhood friend's judgment that when she mentioned a funny script nobody at United Artists wanted to produce, Eisner went right to the telephone and ordered Paramount to pick it up: It became *Airplane,* which cost $4 million and made $40 million. He's the guy who compared *Footloose* to *The Scarlet Letter* and quotes Plato in connection with the Disney Institute. He's the CEO who filmed a sequence for the Disney-MGM Studio Tour wearing a Mickey Mouse watch so that Mickey himself could flash a Michael Eisner watch. He's a guy who reportedly eats popcorn for breakfast. "Whatever he does," producer Larry Gordon once remarked, "he does with 100 percent gusto"—the most Disney-like characteristic of them all.

For Walt, both "magic kingdoms," his Hollywood studio and the theme park, were happy products of his own natural bent. His tinkering with multidimensional camera techniques made real animation possible; his hankering for a fantasy playground for his children produced a modern phenomenon.

Eisner's election to chairman of Walt's company was the result of years of preparation, "schooling," one might say, at three TV networks and a major movie studio. As the Magic Kingdom was to Walt Disney, so Hollywood was to Eisner—the symbol of our dreams, of what life never was really like and what it always should *seem* to be in our hearts. (Eisner opened the Disney-MGM Studios by calling it "the Hollywood that never was and always will be.") Besides, Eisner is a bona fide member of the Disney generation, a classic baby boomer, who knows every cultural touchstone of the last 30 years and who had a hand in creating several of them himself. "My biggest break," he once told *The New York Times,* "was being born in 1942. When I was 21, that was the target audience for everything. When I was 35, the target audience was 35. I always felt and acted as though I was the audience."

While Walt had to sneak his candy money past his father, Eisner probably never even heard the phrase "penny candy" as a child. (In fact, while most of those famous sites re-created in It's a Small World and the World Showcase were only photos to the young Walt Disney, Eisner has visited many of them.) Eisner was raised on Manhattan's Park Avenue and summered in its Westchester County suburbs; he went to a famous Princeton prep, the Lawrenceville School. On his father's side, he was the descendant of a Bohemian émigré named Sigmund Eisner who became the manufacturer of uniforms for both the Boy Scouts and the U.S. Army; his mother was co-founder of the American Safety Razor company and wealthy in her own right. Although he was not a great scholar, he was encouraged to read widely as a youth, and famously sprinkles his conversation with literary and artistic references; he's a fan of modern art and postmodern architecture.

Eisner started his career at NBC as a page, originally a summer job he got through family friends, the Sarnoffs, who owned a large chunk of NBC's parent, RCA. He moved to CBS to take a slot in children's programming, then shifted to ABC in 1966, where he became a protégé of executive Barry Diller. Eisner took over first Saturday morning programming and then prime time, where he launched such successful sitcoms as *Happy Days* and *Welcome Back, Kotter.* And when Diller became chairman of Paramount Pictures, he took Eisner with him as studio president.

"A Deep Sleep Fell Upon the Entire Castle"

The story of the reinvigoration of the Disney Company beginning in the mid-'80s might well be called the Great Movie Ride. It starts with a struggle over the spirit of the company, weaves through threats of buyouts and loss of creative control, and ends up with the company sailing into a beautiful sunset, but with a new king, Michael Eisner—a Hollywood pro rather than a Disney family member—at the helm.

Walt Disney World itself was an unquestionable success: Even though the oil embargo of 1973 and the recession that followed struck hard at the entire region—the Orlando Chamber of Commerce actually organized a sort of fire sale that chopped 10% off the price of all local property—and Disney World had to lay off some employees, it managed to recover in record time. In January 1975 astronauts Scott Carpenter, Gordon Cooper, and Jim Irwin ceremoniously opened Space Mountain, which has remained one of the park's most popular attractions. A few months later the plans for EPCOT were announced, prepping that park's potential audience.

Theme park revenues continued to climb, reaching $434 million by 1980 and jumping even higher after the opening of EPCOT in 1982. Meanwhile, however, the movie division, the company's standard-bearer, was stalling. A dozen animators quit the company over what they said was loss of artistic control, a desertion that was to set back the studio for a decade. By the mid-'80s, the trouble was clearly serious.

Disney's films began taking huge losses at the box office, and rifts developed between old-line Disney loyalists such as Card Walker and Dick Nunis, who thought the company should continue to make the sort of family movies it always had; company director Roy E. Disney, Walt's nephew and head of animation; and Walt's son-in-law (and former football pro) Ron Miller, then president of Walt Disney Productions, who argued that the movie division must change with the times and, more importantly, with the audiences. Miller pushed hard enough to persuade the board to okay a more "adult" movie company, called Touchstone, to release films outside the family mode (although its first film, *Splash,* barely earned its PG rating). Miller even tried to hire Eisner, then president of Paramount Pictures, to rescue Disney, but Eisner refused, accurately concluding the company wasn't "culturally ready," meaning corporately ready, to break with tradition.

By 1984, the company was so weakened and disunited that it became the target of ornate and sometimes interrelated takeover attempts. Roy Disney himself, who had resigned from the board, launched one campaign. Greenmail master Saul Steinberg acquired about 12% of the Disney stock, which scared the board into bringing in the real estate–rich Bass brothers of Texas. Another famous greenmail artist, Irwin Jacobs, also had a chunk of stock in hand, which the Basses bought. Even notorious junk-bond specialists Michael Milkin and Ivan Boesky put in their bids.

It was an expensive battle for the Disney Company, the company Walt swore would never be sold or surrendered. It spent nearly $60 million to buy out Steinberg and took on half a billion dollars in new debt, outraging many of its stockholders. When the dust settled, the dispirited Miller was out; Roy E. Disney was back as head of the animation division; and two film-industry veterans, Eisner, who had resigned from Paramount just ten days earlier, and Frank Wells, vice-chairman of Warner Bros., had been named chairman and CEO respectively. Eisner also brought along Jeffrey Katzenberg, who had been with him at Paramount, to take over as chairman of Disney's movie and TV division.

Roll Film, Roll

Eisner and Wells were opposites that attracted. Though they had similarly quick intelligence and impulsiveness, Wells was more disciplined and steady: Despite his prep school background, Eisner attended an unremarkable Ohio college (Dennison); Wells was a former Rhodes scholar and Stanford law graduate. Eisner slouched; Wells had impeccable carriage. Eisner's suits are custom-made, but often a little askew; Wells would wear denim shirts on informal occasions, but always starched and immaculate. One of the few characteristics they shared was the ability to balance professional and personal ambitions (and a sense of fun): Wells had been president of Warner Bros. until he semi-retired to try climbing the highest mountains on each continent in the world. He and his partners nearly succeeded, in fact, except they failed twice to top Mount Everest.

But Eisner and Wells came to the Disney Company with a single purpose—to regild the studio's tarnished image. First, they assembled a group of stars, something like the old MGM studio system, by signing Robin Williams and Bette Midler, among others, to multimovie contracts. This resulted in a string of broad-audience successes for Touchstone Pictures, including *Down and Out in Beverly Hills* (the company's first R-rated film ever), *The Color of Money, Dead Poet's Society, Good Morning Vietnam, Big Business, Beaches, Pretty Woman, Father of the Bride, The Nightmare Before Christmas, Three Men and a Baby* (Eisner wandered into the French original, *Trois Hommes et un Couffin,* when he saw people on the Champs-Elysées lining up to get in), *Sister Act,* and *What's Love Got to Do With It?* Eisner, Wells, and Katzenberg immediately pushed film-production schedules from 4 to 14 films a year—and then went further by establishing a third film outlet called Hollywood Pictures.

Disney also moved more aggressively into television, not only launching the Disney cable channel but commissioning original Touchstone series, which included such high-grossing hits as Tim Allen's *Home Improvement* and *The Golden Girls.* To further cash in on such Disney and ABC stars as Tim Allen and Jeff Foxworthy, Eisner had Disney's Hyperion Books publish their comic autobiographies, both best-sellers.

Eisner had other good ideas for raising money. He ordered *Pinocchio* to be released on videocassette, well ahead of its regular theatrical re-release schedule (so a new audience would have time to be born), and netted more than $12 million. He discovered that the nearly 500 cartoons and three decades of *Wonderful*

World of Disney episodes in the vaults had never been sold to syndication—an oversight he immediately corrected, raising $40 million in a single month in 1985. And, in what sounds like the most obvious of decisions, he ordered company publicity staffers to come up with an advertising campaign for the theme parks, the first promotion for the parks in the company's history. Attendance immediately jumped 10%.

The Disney company had sniffed out the merchandising possibilities of its shows early, and the mouse ears and Davy Crockett coonskin caps were legends of the business. But merchandising had never been a major concern. Coming from the *Star Trek* and *Happy Days* years, Eisner was far more merchandise-savvy than his predecessors. He was intrigued by the possibilities not merely of T-shirts and ears, but of collectible figurines and limited-reproduction cels and cloned trees. During his administration, Disney merchandise has become one of the most profitable arms of the company. In 1995, more than $15 billion worth of Disney merchandise was sold around the world. A single cel from *Pocahontas* went at Sotheby's auction for close to $21,000.

Wells and Eisner also put plans for movie studio–style attractions on the front burner. Not only was this project a natural match—most of the attractions at the Disney-MGM Studios salute, steal from, or restage movie hits from the company—but there were rumors that Universal Studios was planning to open a similar attraction only a few miles away from Disney

World. Universal's parent company, MCA, was particularly bitter when the Disney-MGM Studios theme park was announced, since the Bass brothers, who rode in to the Disney Company as white knights to stop the greenmail takeover attempts (and wound up with a 25% stake as prize), had been approached by MCA about investing in just such a project.

No matter how well Touchstone was doing, it was the status label, the Walt Disney Films name itself, that Eisner and Wells were most determined to revive. And by 1989, they hit the jackpot: *The Little Mermaid,* which announced the renaissance of Disney animation, grossed $80 million. Other Disney hits included *Aladdin* (which grossed $200 million and spun off a TV series), *Pocahontas, Dick Tracy, Who Framed Roger Rabbit?* (which grossed $150 million), *Honey, I Shrunk the Kids, Hunchback of Notre Dame, Toy Story,* and *The Lion King* (which grossed $1 billion). All these films have been recycled as stage shows or rides or souvenir merchandise at Disney World; this ensures their audiences are continually excited about visiting the park. Even the stage set from the new *101 Dalmations,* which was built outside London, had to be reassembled at Walt Disney World. The stage required two 42-ton shipping containers and a special 20-ton cradle for Cruella's car.

Eisner has even taken the movies a step further by bringing the cartoons to life. In order to put *Beauty and the Beast* on stage, Disney bought and renovated the Palace Theater near Times Square as a family-style theater, as well as the glorious old El Capitan Theatre in Los Angeles. The production budget was an estimated $14 million, and the computer set-up alone cost another $6 million. Putting on the musical cost $400,000 every week, but by the summer of 1996, there were simultaneous productions running in New York, Los Angeles, Washington, D.C., Toronto, Vienna, Tokyo, Osaka, and Melbourne.

Hollywood Pictures, which debuted with *Arachnaphobia,* has become Disney's conduit to the mass market; among its titles have been *Crimson Tide, While You Were Sleeping, Dangerous Minds, The Rock,* and *Mr. Holland's Opus.*

The most daring of the substudios, Miramax, took a giant step into the hip/indie/European market with *Priest, Unzipped,* and *Pulp Fiction.* The latter two films contributed to church groups' denunciation of the company's degenerating values. It also handles "literary" films such as *Emma,* which was released in the wake of the Jane Austen craze.

Corporate Disney still has ambiguous feelings about Miramax. Although his financial and pop-culture clout has resulted in *Pulp Fiction* director Quentin Tarantino's being put in charge of a special "vanity" subdivision called Rolling Thunder, the company wanted to put even more distance between itself and the soft-soft-porn film *Kids,* so that movie was nominally distributed by the once-and-perhaps-future Excalibur Films.

Together, these companies have fulfilled their mission; they have made Disney a name to be reckoned with in the film industry again. In 1994, the film division of the Disney Company reported net profits of nearly $450 million; they were up to $454 million in 1995. In fact, the Disney Co. has so many irons in the fire that last year it announced it would have to cut its movie-making schedule from 40 movies a year to a mere 20, one of which, at last, is *Tarzan*.

The Capital Cities/ABC deal—the second largest commercial merger in U.S. history, behind only the notorious 25-billion-dollar buyout of RJR Nabisco in 1989—brought Disney not only ESPN, but the Arts & Entertainment (A&E) and Lifetime cable networks, several magazine groups including the publishers of *W* and *Women's Wear Daily*, and, in a nostalgic coincidence that would have pleased Walt himself, a group of newspapers including the *Kansas City Star*.

Something like the old *Wonderful World of Disney* is scheduled to return to the air (ABC, of course) with a weekly television series; it will show feature-length Saturday night movies that mix up musicals, comedy, historical dramas, new works, and remakes of old favorites such as *The Love Bug* and *Beverly Hills Family Robinson*.

In addition, the company has gone back into television animation with a vengeance: An estimated 200 cartoon series concepts are in some stage of development, including an animated series based on *101 Dalmations*, *The Mighty Ducks* (crime-fighting, hockey-playing ducks from a parallel universe using the voices of Jim Belushi and Tim Curry), *Gargoyles, Jungle Cubs* (a second-generation spin-off of *The Jungle Book*), and *Quack Pack* (starring Donald Duck as the cameraman for a TV entertainment news show). Disney also acquired Jumbo Pictures (makers of Nickelodeon's popular *Doug*) and Colossal Pictures (Makers of the MTV adult-animation *Liquid Television* and *Aeon Flux* series) to broaden its animation audience range.

"I Can't Wait to Be King"

If Walt was worried about anybody giving away the store, he's happy now: Michael Eisner has been by any standard the best thing to happen to Disney Enterprises since Uncle Walt himself. Charismatic and successful, Eisner never misses a trick and plays most of them close to the vest. In fact, employees say the corporation declined one of the Commerce Department's Malcolm Baldridge Awards for Excellence because the panel would have had to go over too many figures that Eisner preferred to keep private.

Eisner is often referred to as the highest-paid CEO in America, although his actual salary is only $750,000; his contract was designed with lavish stock options and bonuses based on stock performance. In December 1992, a day before new tax regulations were to take effect, he cashed in some of his stock options worth more than $200 million and sold them for a $127 million profit. In fiscal 1994, he made about $10.6 million in salary, bonuses, and stock awards. And in fiscal 1995, he went home with $15.5 million: $750,000 in straight salary, plus an $8 million bonus geared to the company's stock performance and another $6.8 million in stock options.

He thinks big for Disney, as well. After Disney bought Capital Cities/ABC in August, 1995, Eisner enjoyed telling network stars that it was the price—more than $19 billion—that made it attactive. Eisner said that Disney needed to invest so much money to balance its profits that it turned down the CBS network, offered at a mere $5.5 billion, as "too cheap."

Executives, talent agents, producers, and financiers all consider Eisner to have an astonishing instinct for entertainment. Many of his colleagues have staked their careers on his—nearly two dozen Paramount employees followed him to Disney. Former Disney chief financial officer Stephen Bollenbach, now at Hilton Hotels, told *The New Yorker* that Eisner has "an uncanny ability to look at a project, whether it's a film or an animated feature or a theme-park ride, and after a hundred really smart people have screened it he will invariably come in and ask the simplest, smartest question." And Frank Wells, who might have had the top job himself in 1994, reportedly told Disney board members to choose Eisner over himself or former 20th Century-Fox chairman Dennis Stanfill, another candidate, because "good creative judgment is unique, even in this town."

Eisner is not, however, universally admired. His

very creativity and pop instincts have made some more conservative Hollywood insiders nervous. "If he weren't Michael Eisner, you'd think this guy was a lunatic," a safely anonymous studio executive told a reporter. Among his more famous proposals that never made it off the drawing board are a 45-story hotel in the shape of Mickey Mouse and a Winnebago journey across America with his family to get in touch with the people—something like the Clinton/Gore caravan of 1991. In the same interview that he praised Eisner's instincts, Bollenbach also said he micromanages "to a fault," and "the fault is that it physically drains him," a prophetic remark.

Then There Was the Big Breakup

In ten years, Eisner, Wells, Katzenberg, and Co. had successfully transformed Disney, which had less than $1.5 billion in revenue in 1984 and not many promising projects on the horizon, into a company with $10 billion in revenues and an estimated net worth five times that. The value of Disney stock rose by more than 1,000% in the same ten years.

Then came yet another corporate crisis. It began with Wells's death in a helicopter crash in April, 1994. Only a few months later, Eisner was felled by chest pains and underwent emergency heart surgery. Nevertheless, he refused to give Wells's title to Disney Studios chief Jeffrey Katzenberg—reneging, according to Katzenberg, on a promise to do so—so Katzenberg walked out. (Eisner couldn't have been too surprised:

The reason he resigned from Paramount was that he had been passed over as chairman.) According to a story by Robert Sam Anson in the July 1995 *Los Angeles* magazine, Katzenberg's decision not to exercise another year's option cost him $100 million. Katzenberg also persuaded several other key officials, including TV chief Rich Frank, and another handful of animators to go with him.

In a blaze of publicity, Katzenberg joined music tycoon David Geffen and superstar movie director Steven Spielberg in organizing the DreamWorks SKG studio. As soon as DreamWorks went public, Katzenberg, Spielberg, and Geffen each realized paper profits of $567 million. Nevertheless, his pride wounded, Katzenberg sued the Disney Co. for $100 million, claiming the company owed him that much for his work on *Lion King, Aladdin,* and so on.

For the time being, Eisner chose to go it alone, naming himself CEO as well as chairman. Eventually, he hired super-agent Michael Ovitz, head of Creative Artists Agency and a longtime friend, as president of the company.

According to the Anson piece, many other Hollywood executives have been close friends of Eisner, then become estranged—and in some cases become friends again. Geffen, now an Eisner critic because of the Katzenberg break, previously had been an admirer and had discussed partnerships and mergers with Eisner several times over the years. Eisner even explored the idea of Disney buying Geffen Records for $400 million, but the deal was never consummated, and Geffen eventually sold out to MCA. Steven Spielberg, the third member of the DreamWorks team, had also worked with Eisner repeatedly, both at Paramount (*Raiders of the Lost Ark*) and Disney (*Who Framed Roger Rabbit?*).

Barry Diller, Eisner's mentor at ABC and later Paramount Pictures, was one of Eisner's biggest boosters when he first took over Disney. Now at Fox, Diller is no longer speaking to him. MCA chairman Sid Sheinberg has been blunt in his criticism of what he considers Eisner's conning of the media. Several insiders—some eventually hired by Disney or ABC and some not—have been reported to feel manipulated or insulted by clumsy recruiting and corporate in-fighting. And true or not, rumors have flown ever since the Ovitz hiring that Eisner regretted the arrangement. *The New Yorker*'s Ken Auletta quotes a friend of both men who said that Eisner complained, "You know, I knew and vacationed with and dined with Michael Ovitz for 25 years, but I didn't know him at all. That's the mistake I made when I brought him in here. He doesn't know how business operates."

The Greatest Shows on Earth

Reading about Disney projects can be like reading the federal budget: the zeroes tend to lose their impact. Of course the 19-billion-dollar purchase of Capital Cities/ABC is far and away the largest, outside the 50-billion-dollar value of Disney itself; Eisner has lived up to Walt's original Disney World rule: He has never built anything on a small scale.

Disney-MGM Studios, which is about the same size as the Magic Kingdom (with somewhat less concentrated fantasy), cost a relatively modest $300 million, but then it had only about half the number of attractions it has today. The 1994–95 renovation of Tomorrowland cost $100 million. The entire Disneyland in Anaheim is undergoing significant expansion and renovation. And the huge Animal Kingdom park is expected to cost $760 million, a stunning figure that is the largest single budget in Disney history. (Although, if the American history theme park outside Washington, D.C., had passed muster, it would have cost at least $650 million.)

Even individual attractions can be mind-boggling. The 17-minute *Captain EO* 3-D attraction that involved Michael Jackson, Frances Ford Coppola, and George Lucas that was the predecessor to *Honey, I Shrunk the Audience* cost $17 million and was considered extravagant in 1986. "The Twilight Zone" Tower of Terror, added in 1994, ate up $95 million. And the *Extra-TERROR-estrial Alien Encounter*, first opened in 1995, cost about $60 million.

As pointed out in "Pleasure World: Disney for Adults," the company has spent perhaps $400 million on sports acquisitions, franchise bids, and facilities over the last three or four years. Disney's most recent expansion program includes the renovation and doubling in size of the Disney Village Marketplace and the Disney World International Sports Complex, expected to cost $100 million each; construction of the $235 million Coronado Springs Resort and convention center, the Mediterranean resorts, seven or eight other hotels, and a line of cruise ships, the first of which will set sail in January 1998. The town of Celebration (see below) cost $2.5 billion. The Disney Co. has even bought a deserted island in the Bahamas to use as a stopover for its cruises.

Reaching even further into the popular pocket, Disney has a ten-year deal with McDonald's to open 18,700 joint theme restaurants around the world, with options for even more. A deal with Kellogg's is also being finalized. The elaborate Disney Store on Fifth Avenue in New York, with its lavish display of merchandise and its on-site vacation booking office for the resorts, is the flagship of a chain. More Disney memorabilia is available through direct mailings or galleries specializing in animation cels (and authorized reproductions thereof).

Not all Eisner projects are successes, or at least not immediate ones. The record company Eisner did launch after turning down Geffen, called Hollywood Records, was one of his rare miscalculations: One of its first multimillion-dollar contracts was with the glam-rock act Queen, even though its frontman and creative genius Freddy Mercury was already dying of AIDS. Eisner has said Hollywood Records only lost about $10 million, about the same as a disappointing movie release; but other Disney officials told Anson the figure was closer to $75 million.

EuroDisney, a joint venture with the French government, threatened to be Eisner's first disaster. It lost more than $900 million the first fiscal year—1995 was the first year Eisner took home no more than his $750,000 base salary—and had to be refinanced. However, the drain has slowed dramatically, and the Disney Channel is going on French cable, fanning the flame. Even so, the Disney Company's 1995 figures include a profit of $190 million for the theme park/resort division. Unadjusted revenue figures for the first half of 1996 showed the theme park division up another 16%. (Tokyo Disneyland is a franchise operation, so Disney gets only a percentage of revenues.)

Even the Capital Cities/ABC purchase has inspired its share of second-guessing. When the merger was announced in August, 1995, ABC was ranked first in prime-time ratings, nightly news, and morning news, but it has slipped significantly since. ABC also announced in November, 1995 that it would launch a round-the-clock cable news service like CNN's, but had to back out six months later when projections suggested heavy start-up costs (losses of as much as $400 million in its first four years) and falling audience projections.

Nevertheless, if early quarter earnings are a guide, the Disney Company will probably clear $2 billion this year, on revenues of close to $15 billion.

Jam Yesterday, Jam Today

Walt Disney had extraordinary hopes for EPCOT, the Experimental Prototype Community of Tomorrow. He envisioned it as "a showcase for American industry and research," one that would never be completely finished because it would always inspire and absorb the latest technology; a place with schools and churches but without slums ("because we won't let them develop") or landlords (nobody would own property privately); a place with office buildings but no unemployment, no welfare, and no retirement.

In building Celebration, the residential prototype at the west edge of the Disney World property, Michael Eisner has turned another Walt Disney concept around. Celebration is not the ideal community of some high-tech future, but a nice, friendly, old-fashioned American small town. The "Community of Tomorrow," built today, turns out to be . . . yesterday.

It looks nothing like the retro-futuristic pyramids of EPCOT. Instead of being chockful of high-tech gadgets and monorails, it has townhouses, apartment buildings, and garages—all around the back, out of sight. Instead of laboratories and humanely designed factories, it has a school (operated by Osceola County), a complete medical center, a public golf course, and miles of biking and walking trails. Its homes are a relaxed mix of designs: Victorian, Colonial Revival, South Carolina Coastal with long front porches, Mediterranean, some with gingerbread and gables and balconies. All are old-fashioned in a nostalgic sense, nothing as modern or cool as the Swan or Dolphin hotels within the theme park. This is the architecture of the romantic-escape resorts—the Grand Floridian, the Boardwalk, the Dixie Landings.

In fact, along its downtown boulevards, Market Street and Front Street, there are restaurants, shops, a bank, a market, a town hall, and a small cinema—just the sorts of businesses Walt Disney chose for his past-perfect Main Street, U.S.A. Only this time, the apartments over the businesses are real. If Michael Eisner has limited the technological flash of Walt Disney's vision, he has held onto its heart.

Celebration's most Eisner-era elements are its name-brand architects—a dozen firms contributed either to the town's overall planning or to its actual buildings—and its cost. Originally proposed as a middle-income town, it's a little more upscale than that, with houses ranging from about $135,000 to $350,000. Even at that price, there was so much interest that prospective residents had to put down refundable deposits in order to be in a lottery to become one of the first 500 buyers or renters. Eventually, the town may have the 20,000 residents Walt envisioned for EPCOT, not all of whom, contrary to some rumors, are Disney cast members.

Clearly, it is Walt's America that glimmers in Celebration. In a *New Yorker* article by architecture critic Witold Rybczynski, project planner Tom Lewis says Celebration "could have been a second-home community or a resort or a retirement village. Instead, we decided that it would be a place where families would have their primary residences. We wanted it to be a real town"—like Pinocchio, the puppet who had to learn to listen to his heart to become a real boy.

And it was developer James Rouse who in 1963 told the graduating class of Harvard architecture school that Disneyland was "the outstanding piece of urban design in the United States [in its] performance, in its respect for people, in its functioning for people." It was also Rouse, with his own back-to-Main Street new town of Columbia, Maryland, and waterfront revitalization projects in Boston's Faneuil Hall and Baltimore's Harborplace, who pushed for the return of planned communities like Celebration.

CREATIONISM

Backstage and Below Ground

*I*n its seamless melding of function and fantasy, Walt Disney World is a marvel. Elements had to be reconsidered and then re-created; materials had to be perfectly imitated and often improved (fireproofed, strengthened, infinitely replicated); gears and gadgets had to be imagined, engineered, and then—poof!—made invisible. All this became the responsibility of the Imagineers.

In the term "Imagineer" (a contraction of "imagine" and "engineer"), the imagination part comes first, and that's how Walt Disney intended it to work. The Imagineers were assigned to plan, design, engineer, and supervise the whole theme park as they had Disneyland. This is more peculiar than it sounds. The original Imagineers were artists and animators, not builders. They wouldn't have been able to design a building the traditional way even if Walt had wanted them to, which he didn't. To guarantee that they were insulated from any pushy company directors or budget crunchers, Walt created a private company and paid the Imagineers out of his own private pocket. The company was originally called WED Enterprises, in his honor. It was brought into the company in 1964, by which time it was a safely successful and much admired team of writers, computer geeks, researchers, industrial designers, architects, audio and film techies, and so on.

Whereas most real-world architecture is at least conceived with the utilities, light, and traffic flow worked right in, the attractions at Disney World are "drawn" like cartoons, like the preliminary sketches for an animated film; then the pulleys and levers have to be made to fit the picture. So virtually everything about the parks, from the physical structures to the rides to the special effects, was invented as if the rules of practical construction had been suspended. In fact, they had.

Even today, the Imagineers plot rides on storyboards first, getting the "look" not only from the designer's viewpoint but from the passenger's as well. After that a scale model is built and juggled around before blueprints are drawn and the actual logistics are figured out. (Curiosity-seekers should keep their eyes open as they ride through Space Mountain on the Tomorrowland Transit Authority for the model representing the original concept for EPCOT, only about 10 by 20 feet.) When the design for an attraction is fairly set, it's passed over to MAPO (an acronym of "Mary Poppins," whose strange combination of magic and no-

nonsense neatness is the perfect model for the development and manufacturing arm of the company).

Perhaps the best example of Imagineering, inside and out, is Cinderella Castle. First came the "look": Cinderella Castle sums up the Imagineers' bigger-and-better-than-life architectural style (the castle has 10 spires, a Romanesque base, Gothic arches, and Renaissance rococo Bavarian turrets); their pragmatism (the "stone blocks" are made of fiberglass over steel); their obsessive craftsmanship (the five 15-foot mosaic panels in the foyer took a million chips and two years to complete); their whimsy (the "Disney crest" is carved over the great entrance); and their sheer, almost childlike brilliance (the entire five-ton pinnacle of the tower unscrews in case of hurricanes).

Then came the "background." Where the castle now stands, where almost the entire Magic Kingdom now stands, was the rawest swamp—12 feet "deeper" than the park is now—until dredging produced an island and a square mile of Seven Seas Lagoon. Then the wheels and pulleys went in: a suite of apartments originally designed for the Disney family (but never inhabited), a security station in the central tower, and a broadcast center that monitors the progress of the various parades. The second floor houses the restaurant, King Stefan's Banquet Hall. There are three elevators in the Castle, as well as intricate water and ventilation equipment. And, although there are no bats in the Castle belfry, there are pigeons in the palace: One of the top turrets is the "dove cote" (really the loft where the white homing pigeons roost between parades).

But the real magic is down at dungeon level. What seem to be the foundation of the Castle and King Stefan's upstairs banquet hall are actually its second and third stories. Underneath, in the reclaimed swamp, is the Utilidor (for "utility corridor"), a mile of tunnels spoking out in all directions through the Magic Kingdom. At one brilliant stroke, the Utilidor solved three problems: It reduced the amount of fill dirt needed under the park; it allowed all non-magical elements—wiring, garbage, computer operators, and even characters out of costume—to be hidden from sight; and it cut travel time for employees and maintenance staff to scant minutes, because they didn't have to negotiate crowds or public routes.

The Utilidor was constructed above ground, to avoid water seeping in. It probably started out looking like a parking garage. The tunnels, as high as 15 feet, are wide enough to allow tractor-trains of supply carts to pass; the utility lines are marked and within reach; and there are honeycombs of studios and storerooms all around. The hot and cold water pipes, the air conditioning vents and smoke-removal fans, and even the fiber-optic lines and computer hookups are all here in the Utilidor. Pneumatic tubes (the sort that used to carry copy from newsrooms to typesetters in the old days) automatically transfer waste from the surface to garbage trucks in the basement. So guests never see more than a small can of trash, and certainly never any of the dump trucks, which emerge at the ends of the tunnels some distance away. The various tunnels were painted different colors as code for the different theme areas, so that cast members couldn't get lost and show up in the wrong place; theme park pictures were later added for the benefit of color-blind cast members.

The whole thing was then roofed and covered over with eight million cubic yards of dirt dredged from Seven Seas Lagoon, hiding the Utilidor "underground," and the Castle was built on top. The Magic Kingdom, in other words, is several yards above original ground level—a castle in the air.

This underground complex is now the home of many of the DACs and AMCs—Digital Animation Control and Automatic Monitor Control systems—that monitor and control many of the park's environmental systems, including energy consumption, refrigeration, resort and restaurant reservations, and even the Muzak. The computers lie under the Haunted Mansion, in one of the most closely guarded areas. The Utilidor is also one of the major "cast" areas of the theme park. As many as 8,000 employees are there in a day, among them the video and film technicians, tailors, wigmakers and makeup artists, maintenance workers, animators, and computer operators. The Utilidor was a deep secret for many years, but these days, interested guests can see parts of it by taking either of the behind-the-scenes tours called Keys to the Kingdom or Backstage Magic. EPCOT has a much smaller version of a Utilidor, because the pavilions, which, in effect, constitute the outer perimeter of the World Showcase, can be serviced from the back without the guests' knowledge. However, the computer center for that theme park is also below ground, 20 feet under Innoventions East.

• Right before Your Very Eyes . . . •

Imagineering calls for a good eye—and also for knowing how to fool one.

When he was designing Disneyland, Walt had been more focused on eliciting a sense of nostalgia and security, so he built everything to a kind of playhouse scale, five-eighths of its real size. But when it came to Disney World, Walt Disney wanted his ideal Main Street to be a vital, comfortable area for shopping and eating. The stores and restaurants had to be at least close to real size, even if they were crowded. So the Imagineers, drawing on their drawings, used the old artist's trick of artificial perspective: they made the upper stories a little smaller so that they *looked* as if they were stretching even higher into the sky. Therefore, the ground floors are 90% life size, the second floor, 80%, and any third-floor attics even smaller, only 60% real size. This also makes the street seem longer than it actually is: only three football fields from the railroad station to the Castle wall. (Even the speed of the "average guest" was figured into the design—three miles an hour.) But none of the space is wasted; the apparent second-floor rooms are only about three feet deep, and behind the false walls are offices and storage.

Imagineers also have ways of fooling the ear and the nose. In certain rides, as particular cars pass, the "background noises" grow louder in order to help pull the observer into the picture. At the rain forest region of The Land, the animals and birds are cued by sensors to seem alarmed by the human's presence. Sometimes it's just a matter of the details, as with the horseless carriages of Main Street, which have Jeep transmissions but specially-designed mufflers that go *putta-dutta-dut* as if the two cylinders inside were struggling along.

The susceptibility of the human nose is so great that the right scent can sometimes produce three-dimensional hallucinations. Disney's air fresheners are so powerful that they're nicknamed "smellitzers," a joke on howitzer cannons. Sulphur is "fired" into the Universe of Energy, where volcanoes are spewing and dinosaurs are putrifying into fuel oil. Some more cheerful aromas provide atmosphere and encourage consumption at the same time, like the air blown from around the chocolate chip–cookie shop into Main Street.

Lighting effects have always been a part of Walt Disney World—there are several fireworks and special-effects light shows in the park every evening—but they get more high-tech every year. The Magic Kingdom's SpectroMagic parade involves giant prismatic

holographs, military lighting, light-spreading thermo-
plastics, liquid nitrogen "smoke" (a sinuous improvement on the traditional dry ice), electro-luminescent
and fiber-optic technology, in addition to the traditional fluorescent bulbs—a mere 600,000 of them—
and mirrors. The audio is stored digitally on micro-
chips and triggered sequentially by sensors along the
route.

The floating Electrical Water Pageant is Spectro-
Magic on the half shell: a barge parade starring King
Neptune (who does, after all, make an appearance in
SpectroMagic, along with his daughter Ariel) and
cruising around Bay Lake to Handel's "Royal Fireworks Music." IllumiNations, the after-dark show at
EPCOT's World Showcase Lagoon, involves a mixture
of laser lights and fireworks. Disney-MGM Studios
has Sorcery in the Sky, a fireworks display with some
laser additions based on Mickey's famous exploits as
the Sorcerer's Apprentice in *Fantasia*. And by late 1997
(the date has been changed several times), a version of
Disneyland's astonishing Fantasmic! fireworks is scheduled to open in its own amphitheater behind the
Tower of Terror, over its own lagoon.

High Ho, Heigh-Ho, It's Off to Work We Go . . .

Two of the three tallest mountains in Florida are at
Disney World, and neither of them owes anything to
nature. Big Thunder Mountain is 197 feet tall, and
Space Mountain is 180 feet. How they got there is a
story in itself.

Walt Disney World's Big Thunder Mountain has the film-industry pedigree one might expect: It's modeled after Monument Valley, the area director John Ford used in such classic western films as *Stagecoach*. According to the "official" Birnbaum guide to Walt Disney World, it took 15 years to plan and almost 2 to build, requiring layering 4,500 tons of cement over 650 tons of steel and covering that with 5,000 tons of artificial mud and 16,000 gallons of paint. The whole thing weighs 65 tons. After that, the Imagineers called in the strike force to beat the surface with picks, throw stones at it, and toss clods of earth to give it that "weathered" look. The result is so realistic that cast members report having had to dissuade rattled rattlesnakes from trying to find homes there.

Big Thunder Mountain also exhibits a great example of the Imagineer's less expensive ingenuity: The apparently well-aged and "bubbled" exterior of the saloon is the result of mixing plant food into the paint.

Space Mountain, whose shape is a gentle homage to Japan's serene Mount Fuji, is obviously artificial, but its design—72 pre-stressed concrete beams 117 feet long, and gradually decreasing from 13 feet across at the bottom to 4 feet at the top—is equally impressive in a technical way. And Space Mountain's cheap trick? Chocolate-chip cookies, magnified and slightly nibbled, that moonlight as meteorites.

Even leaving out the cookies, the sheer number and variety of materials used in Walt Disney World is astonishing. There are more than 20,000 paint colors, each, along with the items on which they are used, catalogued in the main computer. The mosaics in Cinderella Castle have more than 500 shades of glass, as well as sterling silver and 14-karat gold. And sometimes re-creating a period effect means relearning period techniques. All the costumes for the audio-animatronic Presidents for instance—and each has a spare outfit—were handmade using appropriate sewing methods of the times.

One of the most famous "trees" in Disney World is the one that supports the Swiss Family Treehouse, a classic example of the Imagineers' art. The tree, labeled *Disneyodendron eximus*, or "extraordinary Disney tree," by corporate wags, is 90 feet across, stands 90 feet above the ground, and reaches nearly half as far below. It weighs more than 200 tons, thanks to its steel structure, stucco bark, and concrete roots. It has 1,400 branches, and it is altogether so amazing a feat, and such an obvious symbol of Disney's determination to better nature, that Professor Fjellman named his book *Vinyl Leaves* in honor of its 300,000 plastic attachments.

An even greater tree is to come, one that will dwarf the Swiss Family mansion in its manufacture. The vast Animal Kingdom theme park, scheduled to open in the spring of 1998, will have as its central "castle" a 14-story-tall Tree of Life, a construction so big—its hollow trunk will be 50 feet wide—that it will have a show staged inside. It will also be elaborately carved by Disney artists with pictures of animals, grouped in family and evolutionary patterns.

Some Imagineered effects are necessary concessions to modern life: The Percherons and Belgian draft horses that pull the trolleys along Main Street wear shoes that are steel covered with polyurethane, but the blacksmith at Fort Wilderness works on them the old-fashioned way with anvil and forge. The Mark VII race cars at the Grand Prix Raceway only hit 7 miles per hour in their little track runs, but they do burn real gasoline and cost a respectable $6,000 apiece.

Some environments are real but anomalous, plucked out of their natural settings and brought to Walt Disney World for effect. Even Discovery Island, that little island that captured Walt's heart, had to be entirely re-created by being cleared of scrub; spread with 15,000 cubic yards of soil that was then pushed up into hills and down into pools; topped with 1,000 tons of trees and rocks; and finally planted with hundreds of species of plants and trees from South and Central America, Japan, India, and China.

Sometimes the Imagineers seem to be singing, "Anything you can do, I can do better." Does Old Faithful spout every 64-and-a-half minutes? The Fire Rock geyser at Wilderness Lodge will erupt every hour on the hour except between 10 P.M. and 8 A.M., when somebody might be sleeping.

And sometimes it just seems as though they couldn't take a dare. As famous as Buckminster Fuller's geodesic domes were, almost none were ever built. Spaceship Earth is actually two of them—two domes put together into a *geosphere* that spans 165 feet in diameter and 180 feet in height, with an outer shell made of 954 aluminum triangles and a sort of inner tube, 20 feet smaller, of steel and waterproof lining. The globe weighs 8,000 tons.

Most Imagineering is a strange combination of real and surreal, or Ur-real. The original 72 horses on Cinderella's Golden Carrousel were hand-carved 80 years ago in elaborate detail by Italian employees of the Philadelphia Toboggan Company. But by the time Disney scouts found them in Olympic Park in Maplewood, New Jersey, in the mid-'60s, layers of paint had obscured the fine work. The horses were stripped and repainted (all as white as a princess' steed, but each with an individually painted harness), their legs repositioned, and 18 more carved in exact imitation.

At Madame Lafayette's Parfumerie in Liberty Square, fragrances are custom-mixed to the patron's liking, but any one can be reordered because its "unique" formula is computerized. The birds and animals of the Jungle Cruise are all audio-animatronic, but the sounds were carefully recorded in Africa and South America for authenticity.

The plants in Living with the Land are all plastic; the tree trunks and branches meticulously molded from living trees; and the blades of grass a fire-retardant blend of glass and rubber, but the "rain," which precipitates out of the air from the artificially maintained humidity, is in at least some sense real. In the greenhouses where the experimental and hydroponic gardening techniques are displayed, the plants and the water are real, but the soil is artificial. The Swiss Family Treehouse tree is man-made, but the Spanish moss hanging on it is real.

The buffalo rifles in the Frontierland Shootin' Gallery are genuine Hawkins 54-calibers, but they have been modifed to shoot infrared beams. Some of Main Street's wooden planks are really fiberglass, but the wooden pegs are real. Much of the antique mining equipment on Big Thunder Mountain is real, and the "rust" on the rest is half-real: It's ground-up rust bonded in resin to the top of rust-proof steel bolts. The whitewash on the fence at Tom Sawyer Island looks real enough, but it's actually liquid chalk. Because of this, as many kids as want to can paint every day, and maintenance staff can hose the fence clean every night. The totem poles outside Wilderness Lodge are authentic Pacific carvings, but the "hot spring" that feeds the swimming pool and the geyser are artificial. The colonial-style shell of *The American Adventure* isn't colonial and the AudioAnimatronic Americans aren't real, of course—but the 110,000 bricks are, made by hand from Georgia clay.

The lake that holds the 20,000 Leagues Under the Sea ride is a typical conglomerate of natural and artificial elements. The shell, which holds 11-and-a-half million gallons of water, is steel and fiberglass; the rocks are steel covered with plastic; and the starfish, barnacles, and mollusks are all cast-fiberglass copies.

River Country's rocks are a mix of plaster-covered steel, fiberglass, cement, and real rocks "imported" from Georgia and the Carolinas (the same rocks used in the Japan Pavilion in EPCOT).

Even more elaborate a construction is EPCOT's "Caribbean coral reef" in The Living Seas. It's a 28-foot-deep concrete tank, with a "reef" made of fiberglass and silicone. It is filled with over 5-and-a-half million gallons of imitation sea water that has to be constantly recycled and filtered to maintain its various salts and minerals in a sort of reverse version of a swimming pool pump. Here at least the starfish and such are real, but the coral is not. Nor is it real in the Pacific coral lagoon tank or any of the other pools in the pavilion, and some of the coral-dwelling fish have to be diverted from eating it. The living fish, hundreds of varieties of them, eat frozen fish, hundreds of pounds of them.

This mix of simulation and authenticity is an in-joke in a park built on the movie industry, such as Disney-MGM Studios. Building facades, perspective effects, and false backgrounds are the reality of film. While EPCOT offers half-sized but faithful replicas of such landmarks as the Gate of Heaven in Beijing, a Mayan temple in Mexico, or the Doge's Palace in Venice, Disney-MGM offers a full-scale version of Grauman's Chinese Theatre, but only a couple of feet thick. At the Magic Kingdom, the subtle forced perspective of building looks real to the eye; at Disney-MGM, the backdrops of New York City are painted in visibly forced perspective that is obvious to the eye.

And because the Disney-MGM Studios is all about movie-making, the puns get double-layered. For instance, at the *Indiana Jones Stunt Spectacular,* all the apparent crew members, the prop people, the sound techies, etc., are part of the show, just actors. The real sound people are out of sight—and even they aren't really "sound people" any more either, but computer techies in charge of fully automatic disks and electronic cueing.

Catastrophe Canyon, a set-up version of a special effects scene of an earthquake and fire, seems like a mirror version of Big Thunder Mountain until passengers are shown the gas pipes that supply the "fire." (But it's highly unlikely that in this litiginous age— and in this incredibly expensive set-up—that the real gas pipes are exposed to potential tampering or damage). The supposedly real-life experiments in sound editing, blue-screen formatting, and model shooting that are part of the MGM Studio Tour are only semi-real, temporary overlays that are never really mixed into the digital production. The animators in the studio are obviously real, but the Oscars in the lobby are reproductions.

The see-through robot at the *Extra-TERRORestrial Alien Encounter,* who looks like a combination of C-3PO and the old "Visible Body" models, is a real audio-animatronic figure but a fake robot, since at least some of the wiring is cosmetic.

Now that virtual reality has entered the picture, the combination of "real" and "unreal" is even more complicated. At Eclectronics in the Innoventions pavilion at EPCOT, you can take a virtual reality tour guided by an audio-animatronic host; or check out the Walt Disney Imagineering Laboratory and their virtual reality plans, based on the animated *Aladdin,* for a future fantasy ride. That's a virtual-reality visit with a virtual being—or virtually real virtual-reality visions of a virtually real theme park.

"I Want to Be a Real Boy"

Walt Disney's long effort to develop lifelike robots goes back to the '30s, when he tinkered with hydraulically manipulated giant dolls that sat on top of their machinery like huge, clumsy jacks-in-the-box. His obsession also suggests a certain bittersweet element to one of his best-loved cartoons: *Pinocchio,* the story of a marionette (and his aging, avuncular creator) who becomes more and more human until he finally becomes a real boy.

From the early animal robots that had only one or two movements (hippos that opened their mouths and sank back, etc.), to the elaborate C-3PO-like host at the *Alien Encounter* and his Robin Williams parody over at *Timekeeper,* Disney's AudioAnimatronics have become more and more impressive. The Alien itself is no slouch, as a matter of fact, and an in-house rumor has it that the audio-animatronic dinosaurs being prepared for Animal Kingdom are breathtaking.

The AudioAnimatronics are first modeled on a

small scale in clay, then a second full-size model is made. Next comes a hollow plastic body (a sort of test run for the high-tech innards), followed by a plastic body molded from the clay to make a "skin" of a vinyl synthetic called Duraflex that, as its name suggests, stretches and flexes. The compressed-air hoses and valves that move the body are the same as those used in space suits. Tiny electric relays are installed around the corners of the mouths and eyes to increase the realism of facial expressions. Then, just as live actors and actresses are filmed acting out cartoon scripts so that their animated versions can be drawn as exactly as possible, real people are studied and turned into computer film so that the AudioAnimatronics' movements can be programmed in as a flood of electronic bytes. In a way, it's another virtual reality game, except that the perceived video is "memorized" by the robot.

Although they can be slow and stiff, the AudioAnimatronics fascinate their audiences. One man entering *The Hall of Presidents* for what was clearly the third or fourth time, insisted, "I want to get down close enough to see their lips move—I've always been too far back."

It isn't just their lips that have to move, or that require astonishing leaps of technology to do so. In *The American Adventure*, during which the robot figures enter, exit, row, write, and ride horseback, the characters—including three or four separate Ben Franklins and Mark Twains, each with different speeches—are grouped along a vast moveable underground stage. Nicknamed the "war wagon," it rolls back and forth from side to side in order to hoist the sets and animatronic speakers into place. (Ben doesn't really walk up the stairs: he's gently boosted up one step at a time.) The wagon weighs 175 tons, so great a weight that the surface beneath it has 300-foot-deep pilings. If you sit close enough, you can hear the gears turning and the poor thing creaking. But then, that's what earthquakes are, too—the sets moving around.

Bigger, Better, Faster, Scarier

There is a moment during the new *Extra-TERROR-estrial Alien Encounter* ride in which the megalomaniacal multibillionaire from another galaxy, president of XS Tech, says with irresistible flourish, "If something can't be done with XS, it shouldn't be done at all." It sounds like an in-house joke: After the first time Disney CEO Michael Eisner sat through the $60 million ride that, theatrically speaking, lets the Alien loose to snack on the strapped-in passengers, Eisner sent it back to the Imagineers' drawing board because it wasn't scary enough. (The improvements included the hot breath on the back of passengers' necks, the "blood" that sprays the room, and the night vision film.)

That doesn't happen very often, because Disney Imagineers are usually on the leading edge of special effects. Body Wars in EPCOT and Star Tours in Disney-MGM Studios use flight simulators, adapted from aircraft simulation training installations, to produce the sensations of take-off, rapid transit, landing, turbulence, or even free fall and collision. Each simulator can be adapted into a 40-seat theater and perform 26 movements that, synchronized with the films, "persuade" the inner ear of acceleration and imbalance, although the actual give is only a few feet in any direction. Star Tours and Body Wars each use four of these simulators, at a cost of a half-million dollars apiece. And since the video and synchronized effects of the simulators—the script—can be updated without much structural work, the next generation of rides will almost certainly involve computer-generated virtual reality technology.

Disney is already using virtual reality to remarkable effect—not only keeping up with the art but often pushing it forward. The '90s' three-dimensional effects of *Captain EO* were a revelation to many, but the VR punch of *Honey, I Shrunk the Audience* is a leap beyond that. Instead of the old red-green glasses, the new technology involves a sort of two-eyed camera, one whose simultaneously filming lenses are about two inches apart, like human eyes, and the film is a special high-speed format. Unlike *EO*, in which the effects were truest in the center, the new technology makes the holographic images convincing from any place in the room. Combined with smoke, fiberoptics, water "sliming," and moveable seats—not to mention little feathery "mouse tails" underneath the chairs—it's pretty amazing. In fact, we defy anyone to resist flinching from the breaking glass.

Apparent movement doesn't require much real space. The "descent" into The Living Seas' "Sea Base Alpha," which seems to be about 50 feet and takes 30 seconds, actually is only a couple of inches. It is made to feel deeper by vibrations, lighting changes, bubbles that suggest pressure changes, and scenery that rises—fooling the mind just the way a car rolling forward next to you can make you feel as if you're rolling backward. In the *Carousel of Progress*, the "ride," in this case the stage, doesn't move at all: The audience rotates around it. And some of the super-wide screen films, like the 360° Circle-Vision film segment of the *Timekeeper*, were shot at such speed (in this case, up to 60 miles per hour along the bobsled run) that your stomach may also shoot the hairpin curve.

When it comes to creating scary rides with real movement, however, speed is of the essence, because it exaggerates the degree to which the rider feels off balance, cut loose, or out of control.

The cars in Space Mountain hit about 28 miles per hour; Splash Mountain reportedly works up to a top speed of 40, with a 52-foot drop at a 45° angle. But neither of those comes close to the stomach punch provided by the 13-story deadfall drop in "The Twilight Zone" Tower of Terror, which some people have guessed hits 45 miles per hour.

The race is on all over the World. The Rock-and-Roller Coaster being considered for Sunset Boulevard at Disney-MGM Studios will wind through the fretboard of a huge guitar, the hole in the center of a 45-

rpm record (if anyone remembers those by the time the ride opens), and through one of the "O"s in a replica of the "HOLLYWOOD" sign to be built on the hillside overlooking the studios. Appropriately enough, the ride will also hit 45 miles per hour. But at least there, passengers will be riding in pink big-fin Cadillacs. "Skiers" running the 120-foot drop at Blizzard Beach are said to hit 60 mph in only their bathing suits.

The new Test Track ride, which will be the centerpiece of the renovated GM World of Motion Pavilion at EPCOT when it reopens in 1997, is expected to go even higher. Disney officials say the vehicles, which will take passengers through a one-mile simulation of the all-terrain, all-weather testing to which manufacturers subject new cars, will approach highway speed—which, at least on the Florida Turnpike only minutes away, is 75 miles per hour. Not only that, but there is an outside section of curved track (visible from the backstage parking lot if you take certain behind-the-scenes tours) and a crash test in which you may bust through the "wall" of the building. Got your seatbelt on?

THE FUN FACTORY

"Whistle While You Work"

"*I*magineering" Walt Disney World is a mammoth and continual undertaking, but nobody ever said it wasn't fun. The Disney creative engineering team was dosed with the original pixie dust—Walt's personal affection and trust—and their dedication to his vision includes building in the whimsy, the warmth, and the sly film and other cultural references that provided visual puns in even Disney's earliest cartoons. Animation was never kid stuff, not really, and aside from the specific design challenges, the Imagineers were determined to build just those sorts of little puns and pleasures into the park. Besides, it was more fun for them.

Many of the original Imagineers, as well as some of the executives, have hidden "credits" around the park. The joke tombstones at the Haunted Mansion refer to art directors, Imagineers, and scriptwriters; the five singing busts in the graveyard, the heads in the library, and the fortune teller in the crystal ball represent animators, voice-over artists (including Paul "Boris" Badenov and Thurl "Tony the Tiger" Ravenscroft), wardrobe designers, and illusionists. Names on crates at the Jungle Cruise and on shops along Main Street are also tributes: Dick Nunis, chief of operations during the building of the park and then president, is said to run the gym. The names "Bill Davis," one of Disney's pseudonyms, and Bob Foster, one of the real estate attorneys who managed the great Orlando purchase, are on the sign of the hilariously frank "Pseudonym Real Estate Development Co." There's also an M. T. Lott Real Estate Investments firm. Ub Iwerks got a visual pun in the sign for "Iwerks-Iwerks Stereoscopes."

Walt's name is on the second floor of the ice cream parlor, facing the Castle; brother Roy is listed as offering sailing lessons. Onetime Walt Disney Productions president Card Walker moonlights as "Psychiatrist and Justice of the Peace." Imagineer Roger E. Broggie has a train named after him, as do Walt, his wife Lillian (aka "Lilly Belle"), and Roy Disney. A note on the wall at the *Carousel of Progress* says, "Marty called— wants changes!", a reference to chief of Imagineering, Marty Sklar. In the same ride, among the pictures of the teenagers' movie idols of the '40s, is a photo of Walt Disney.

For all its very up-to-date corporate outlook, the Disney company has made at least one totally sentimental move in honor of Walt Disney World's first quarter-century: The longtime park logo, in which the capital "D" was squared off to enclose the globe with the Mickey Mouse ears, has been quietly replaced by Walt Disney's own signature, with the word "World" added on. Calculated to advertise the company's old-fashioned family values? Maybe—but you gotta like it anyway.

• He's Everywhere! He's Everywhere! •

Walt Disney never stopped reminding his employees that they owed their kingdom to a Mouse, but if Mickey cast a long shadow over the company, it was a beloved one. One of the most endearing hobbies the Imagineers have is hiding Mickeys—Mickey "logos," made up of one large circle and two smaller ones at 10 and 2 o'clock; Mickey "ears" like Mouseketeer hats (half-circles with smaller circles above); heads with pointed hats, from the "Sorcerer's Apprentice" segment of *Fantasia*; and Mickey silhouettes, with little raisin noses (and both ears, since Mickey's auditory appendages somehow pivot so as to be roundly visible from every angle).

These are not the intentional or "blatant" Mickeys such as the water tower (the Earful Tower) or Mickey topiaries; nor are they "decor" Mickeys, printed on plates or programs. These are shapes you could (and probably will) pass right by at least once in the blur of park life. They are overhead, underfoot, in sets, in shops, in shadows, in shrubs—even, if you stay in some of the hotels, in the patterned wrapping of rolls of toilet paper. They are tiny, huge, drawn, three-dimensional, in films, and in facades. They're in the theme parks, the resort hotels, the restaurants, and even in some of the recreational areas. According to cast legend, there is at least one Hidden Mickey in every ride and amusement in the entire World.

They range from the fairly obvious floral plantings, like the plot in the middle of the Main Street entrance; to the slightly more subtle, like the three-lobed cactus target in the Frontierland Shootin' Gallery; to the most elaborately constructed shadows, like the one that appears as a Lost Boy swoops by in Peter Pan's Flight. If you count the Mickeys in various fence railings, bas-relief patterns, café transoms, and so on, there are thousands; count the carpets and those laundry supplies and who knows?

Nobody does know, in fact, exactly how many there are. Some are reported on Disney-freak World Wide Web sites and then "flamed" as wishful thinking; some are erased by renovations; some are on such deep background only certain cast members are ever in a position to see them. (Any time you're waiting in line, ask the nearest cast member to show you one. Chances are at least one is within sight.)

Finding Hidden Mickeys is a full-time hobby with some fans. The Disney Channel's *Walt Disney World Inside Out* program has finally acknowledged the fascination visitors have with the puzzles, and a couple of Web sites are devoted to listing only those "vanished"

Mickeys that have been renovated out of existence
(not to mention the several pages devoted to record-
ing new ones). The following are some examples that
show both the humor and the fondness the Imagineers have for their mascot.

Some are built into ride "sets": In the *Carousel of
Progress,* the mother's computer screen flashes a
Mickey screen saver (and there are Mickeys and Disney references all over the Christmas scene), and in
the Tomorrowland scene where a woman is having
her hair done, there is a Mickey head on her belt
buckle. Some are very fleeting—visible only from
certain angles or when doors or windows open or
close—like the one cast at certain times by the light
pole between the Mad Hatter's Tea Party ride and the
Grand Prix raceway. In the film at The Land, the
woman testing the pollution in the Willamette River
is wearing sunglasses in which is reflected a cameraman in a Mickey T-shirt. (You need good eyes for
many of these.)

Some Hidden Mickeys are so basic a part of the
Imagineering scheme and so vast in scope that they are
only visible to VIPs flying overhead, or at least study-
ing blueprints and maps. Among the largest Mickeys
is the one formed by the central plaza of MGM Studios, with its two little garden "eyes," the curved smi-
ley entrance to Grauman's Chinese Theatre, and the
round Echo Lake and Brown Derby restaurant "ears."
Others include the Mickey-shaped forest of more
than 30,000 trees west of the Magic Kingdom; a

triple-loop interchange off Interstate 4; a combination of concrete and bush plantings at the Contemporary Hotel, visible only at penthouse level; and the World Showcase Lagoon at EPCOT. Look back toward the AstroOrbiter in Tomorrowland from the Skyway's midpoint transfer station, and the building becomes his head.

Until Mickey's Toontown Fair was wedged in between Fantasyland and Tomorrowland, the entire Magic Kingdom was shaped like Mickey's head. In fact, it's rumored that from on high, the three primary theme parks still suggest a Mickey-esqe roundness (with EPCOT and the Disney-MGM Studios as the head and the Magic Kingdom forming one ear), but that, as they say on the Web, is a contested sighting.

Some Hidden Mickeys are structural in nature. The Haunted Mansion's "stretching" elevator and the two smaller holding rooms that open onto it is a Mickey. There's a huge "dent" in the Cambodian ruins of the Jungle Cruise that is Mickey's silhouette, as well as three "lava rocks" way back in the forest that few guests have ever seen. There are three round-headed palms alongside the Monorail near EPCOT, shrubbery outside and below the Delta Dreamflight, three rocks on the ground in The Land, and, in some areas, patterns drawn by landscapers with rakes.

A couple of Mickeys are literally in the stars: There's an entirely new constellation of diamonds in the ceiling of Spaceship Earth, and the outline of Steamboat Willie is "routed" in the star map over the register in the Star Trader shop at Disney-MGM Studios. Another Hidden Mickey is in the SpectroMagic parade: The mirror balls on Mickey's float, designed to reflect just so in the mirrors, become a Mickey from both left and right. Among the many in the Haunted Mansion are: the eye with the three "pupils" in one of the holographic busts that watch you pass, the setting of three plates on the ghostly banquet table, and on the upper right-hand "turret" as you face the front door (the side away from the ride entrance). The three-circle design is built into the railing around Cinderella Castle (making the shadows Mickeys); the second-story trim, along with the trim over the Traders of Timbuktu shop in Adventureland, are repeated Mickeys.

The Grand Prix ride has a diversionary, blatant Mickey in the painted mural and a genuine Hidden Mickey, created by the rounded grille of the race car on the pedestal with two painted circles behind it. There are several in the *Extra-TERROR-estrial Alien Encounter,* beginning with the hieroglyphics on the poles along the waiting queue: In each cartouche-like set, the Mickey appears as the sixth icon down on the right. There are a lot in the Pirates of the Caribbean, too: the locks on boxes, the lamp bases in the treasure room, and even some of the shadows have ears. The Columbia Harbour House has a trio of ancient "world maps" on the wall, each perfectly round, and there's a Mickey-shaped island east of Australia in the Dreamfinder ride at EPCOT. There are stacked bar-rels on Splash Mountain, a fan in the barn, a knotted rope in the kitchen, and three kettles hanging on the wall, as well as a profile stamped into the purple rocks near where the porcupine plays vibes on the tortoise. A Mickey silhouette is chipped into the street of MGM's New York alley near the locksmith's store; the gauges on Rosie the Riveter's welding torch at Rosie's Red Hot Dogs form a Hidden Mickey; and a whole pattern of them is woven into the carpet in the waiting area of *Honey, I Shrunk the Audience* at EPCOT.

The Spaceship Earth ride is full of Hidden Mickeys —from the Greek's tunic brooch to the treasure box lock. But the sweetest of them is among the most secret: On the pedestal behind the sleeping monk is a book inscribed with the names of Walt Disney, Mickey Mouse, and various Imagineers. (Mickey's name is a subset of the game, and in much sparser supply when you eliminate the intentional ones.) Veins in the sign over the entrance to Body Wars make a Mickey. In *The Making of Me,* the balloons at the prom where Martin Short's parents meet are Mickey-shaped. The blueprint rolls are stacked two on one in Innoventions East. At the Maelstrom ride at the Norway Pavilion, one Viking in the mural is wearing Mickey Mouse ears for a helmet; there are three red floats piled together; and three of the holes in a hollow tree trunk look extremely suspicious.

In the "Twilight Zone" Tower of Terror, the little ghost girl is carrying a 1930s Mickey doll; the boiler's gauges form a triple circle; and the sheet music in the library refers to Mickey in the titles. The overhead tapestries in the Polynesian resort are a Mickey print. The horses on the model carousel in the Boardwalk lobby have Mickey-shaped spots. The five paintings behind the reception desk at the Disney Institute all have Hidden Mickeys. There have been more than two dozen spotted at Wilderness Lodge, and so on.

There is even a sort of second-generation Hidden Mickey game that involves the films of Steven Spielberg and George Lucas, both of whom grew up Walt Disney fans. (Remember that "When You Wish Upon a Star" is the climactic music of *Close Encounters of the Third Kind.*) When the rear half of the plane that was used in *Casablanca* was bought and moved to the *Indiana Jones Stunt Spectacular* at Disney-MGM Studios, Imagineers drilled and reshaped three holes in the metal to get a Mickey into the mix. Pharaoh Mickey (and cup server Donald) are in the hieroglyphs of the *Raiders of the Lost Ark* segment of the Great Movie Ride, as are robots C-3PO and R2D2. There are several Hidden Mickeys in Lucas's Star Tours: One of the baby Ewoks is carrying a stuffed Mickey toy, and the first G2 robot is wearing a Mickey Mouse watch.

• More Games Imagineers Play •

The hide-and-seek is beginning to spread beyond Mickey and the occasional Donald. Lucas himself makes a couple of guest appearances: Visitors waiting to enter Star Tours hear a call for "Egroeg Sacul," George Lucas spelled backwards. A hazardous materials truck has a registration number that is, or at least was, the phone number for Lucasfilms and license plate number THX 1138, the name of an early Lucas film. These are the Hidden Georges. He makes an intentional appearance during the Disney-MGM Studio Tour as well.

Another, though less common, adult game hidden throughout Walt Disney World is the literary quotation, a sort of *Name That Tune* as you go along. For instance, the Greek being quoted by the classical actors in Spaceship Earth is from Sophocles' *Oedipus Rex,* and the book in the Renaissance section is Virgil's *Aeneid.* Birnbaum says that the type on Gutenberg's press is in fact movable, and the page he is proofing is a replica of one from the Huntington Library's original Bible.

There's one other type of hidden tribute woven throughout the park: what might be called "hidden flickies," or movie and TV clips slipped without fanfare into other sets in addition to the intentional clips. Many are Disney's own: The Little Mermaid is among the items dumped into the "brain" at Cranial Command; a hidden Pocahontas has been spotted in the newsreel at Space Mountain; in *The Making of Me,* the parents go in to see *20,000 Leagues Under the Sea,* which also appears in Spaceship Earth; the pre-show of *Extra-TERROR-estrial Alien Encounter* has film from *Mission to Mars,* the show that the *Encounter* replaced; and bits from *The Black Hole* are visible at Dreamfinder's home. There are also the Lucas and Spielberg references mentioned above. But some are even stranger: The music at "The Twilight Zone" Tower of Terror, in addition to the familiar da-da-da-da, also includes the ghostly theme from *The Shining.* Heeeeeere's Mickey!

One great sight gag is at Pleasure Island—the rotating giant dinosaur next to Planet Hollywood in Pleasure Island: It's a dead ringer for Earl Sinclair, the Jackie Gleason–like *pater tyrannosaurus* of the cult classic satire *Dinosaurs,* which cheerfully lampooned modern television and entertainment in best Jim Henson style. RIP, Rex.

The last concentrated group of tributes is built into "The Twilight Zone" Tower of Terror, and these, not surprisingly, are to the Rod Serling TV series itself. Imagineers viewed every one of the 156 original episodes at least twice, and most of Serling's introductions more often than that, before piecing together the video. And "Twilight Zone" memorabilia is displayed throughout the ride—enough to spark a new Hidden Serling chase among his fans. Some of the props displayed in the building are the broken glasses from "Time Enough at Last," the heartbreaking story in which book lover Burgess Meredith survives a nuclear holocaust only to drop his only eyeglasses; the alien "cookbook" from "To Serve Man"; and a robot miniature invader.

Incidentally, watch Serling's hands closely; since

Walt Disney's lung cancer converted him to a critic of smoking, Serling's omnipresent cigarette has been erased from the film—as has a cigarette in the picture of Walt with Laurel and Hardy on display in "The Disney Story" in the Magic Kingdom.

Follow the Yellow Brick Road

Another sort of tribute the Imagineers paid Walt Disney was to embed his road map of the Magic Kingdom into the layouts of both EPCOT and Disney-MGM Studios.

As discussed in depth in "America's Adventures in Wonderland," Walt Disney intended every guest at the Magic Kingdom to begin a visit by passing through the circuit of the railroad, the physical transition from one world to another, into Main Street. This same controlled passage is built into EPCOT, only this time the palace is Earth itself, in the glittering form of Spaceship Earth, and the monorail loop replaces the railroad. Cinderella Castle and Spaceship Earth, to make the parallel even stronger, are exactly the same height: 180 feet tall.

At Disney-MGM Studios, you still have to take the pilgrimage route along Hollywood Boulevard, which becomes the "main street" of the film industry. Here the temple at the end of the ritual path is Grauman's Chinese Theatre, the site of all those legendary star-studded movie premieres—and it makes for another Imagineer joke: Grauman's (now Mann's) Chinese Theatre was the spot where starlets used to put their feet in concrete, if not glass slippers, so it was really the Cinderella Castle of the silver screen. If you look around, you'll find Cinderella's size 3 or so right there.

Also, perhaps as a tribute to Walt's own fascination with explorers and maps, each of the main avenues in the three parks are laid out on a north-south axis.

There is one striking difference between Hollywood Boulevard and the other "main streets" in the Magic Kingdom and EPCOT: It looks lived-in. Paints are faded, or rather mixed to look aged. Similarly, while Walt's beloved Main Street is immaculately, obsessively clean, the New York street set at Disney-MGM includes theatrical grime and even graffiti—dirt that has to be maintained just as meticulously as the spotless paint of Main Street. The Big City, apparently, isn't quite as magical as the Small Town.

• "Once Upon a Time . . ." •

After the look, the location, the levers and gears, and the special effects, storyboards still have one other essential element: the story. And although the scripts of the thrill rides become obvious, the Disney folks still like to have a fable for every feature.

Big Thunder Mountain is so named because of a Disney-invented legend in which a sacred mountain in Wyoming would bellow in warning whenever "white men" stole the gold in it. The town down the slope, Tumbleweeds, was flooded when rainmaker Cumulus Isobar got carried away.

Pleasure Island is the remnant of the resort estate of Merriweather Adam Pleasure, a turn-of-the-century shipping magnate and world traveler who was lost at sea in 1939. His no-account sons let the island fall into disrepair, and Disney executives aboard the *Empress Lilly* riverboat saw it and decided to restore it. (It is supposedly Merriweather Pleasure's souvenirs that are collected at the Adventurers Club.)

Typhoon Lagoon was a resort swamped by a you-know-what, followed by an earthquake and a volcanic eruption, which should have been enough material for even the dimmest Imagineer. In fact, it comes off sounding like a combination of *Gilligan's Island* and *Jaws*. A sign near the entrance tells the story of "the furious storm [that] roared 'cross the sea." Instead of the S.S. *Minnow*, you have the shrimp boat *Miss Tilly* out of "Safen Sound." It got stranded like Noah's Ark on the top of Mount Mayday and periodically spouts water from its smokestack like a beached whale. The two speed slides, cut into the landscape by the "earth-quake," drop 50 feet at about 30 miles an hour. The artificially controlled surf tops out at 4-and-a-half feet and strikes the "shore" about every 90 seconds— thanks to another cleverly simple mechanism: a set of holding tanks that fill up, dump the water all at once (creating the tsunami), and fill up again. The most intriguing detail is the Shark Reef, another artifical coral reef populated by harmless bonnethead and leopard shark; free snorkel equipment is on-hand for a Peter Benchley experience.

Blizzard Beach is a sort of "meltdown," the remains of a failed ski resort on the slopes of Mount Gushmore. (You first have to buy that a freak ice storm dumped a mountain of snow in Florida, but then anything goes in this World.) Theme details include slalom-like flumes and a chair lift that offers a view so spectacular that it's worth the ride even if you don't want to drop from the 120-foot-high summit on your toes. (The slide is 350 feet long, and "passengers" top out at about 60 mph.) There's also a kids' training course with "icebergs" to cross, and so on.

Even the less elaborate set-ups have little stories tossed in. There is a wedding ring embedded in a brick near the exit of the Haunted Mansion, and various reports have it that (1) the ring belonged to Master Gracey (the mansion owner), who tossed it out because the "body" hanging in the stretch room is his fiancée, who committed suicide the night before the wedding; (2) the ring belonged to his wife, who found herself trapped in the room and went insane; (3) Gracey was a sort of Bluebeard, and the ring belonged to his "last" wife, who murdered Gracey and then threw herself off the roof. Incidentally, "Master Gracey," whose headstone is one of those at the entrance, refers to Yale Gracey, one of the Imagineers mentioned above.

Disney also makes fun of itself, at least sometimes. If it begins to rain, the guides on the Jungle Cruise boats and the Mike Fink keelboats often say something like, "It's not real rain. It's just another

Disney special effect." And an *Orlando Sentinel* reporter spotted a pumpkin that fell off the table during a carving contest; it almost instantly acquired a barricade and a wry marker that read: "Please excuse our mess, this pumpkin is being refurbished for your future enjoyment."

PLEASURE WORLD

The Adult Industry

*B*asketball phenomenon Michael Jordan, Super Bowl quarterback Joe Montana, tennis king Pete Sampras, World Series pitcher Orel Hershiser, even Miss America—the famous "I'm going to Walt Disney World!" campaign has made it official: It's not just for kids anymore.

Walt Disney may have begun with his children in mind, but Michael Eisner is a certified baby boomer, with decades of self-indulgence and conspicuous consumption to use as a market barometer. So the vast majority of attractions, rides, resort amenities, and new programs introduced into the theme parks over the last decade have been aimed at grown-ups. Even those that were intended to please the adolescents and teenagers, such as the water parks and thrill rides, have been wildly successful among the adults as well.

It's the greening of Disney World—physically and economically—and in some cases the graying as well.

You can see it in the Disney Institute, a modern Chautauqua town that takes all those gourmet magazines, sports challenges, Martha Stewart shows, and other intimidating yuppie hobbies, and condenses them into two-hour classes. You can hear it in the music (golden oldies and C&W, the two hottest formats in modern radio), see it in the bars, and spot it on the massage menu. You can see it on the restaurant menus, too, although Disney food seems to be one of the few things Imagineers can't make better. You can measure it in the increasing number of recreational activities available at the resorts: golf, tennis, croquet, swimming, boating, fishing, skiing, weight-lifting, running, roller-blading, volleyball, biking, even parasailing and rock climbing. (It's no surprise that the first Walt Disney Resorts outside park grounds are at golf and tennis havens: Vero Beach, Florida, and Hilton Head, South Carolina.) You can also figure it into the number of convention centers and executive retreats built into the resorts.

But, by far, Disney's biggest and shrewdest push of modern times is into the spectator sports arena. In 1992, Disney paid $50 million, half in franchise fees, half against prospective losses to the L.A. Kings, for the National Hockey League's expansion team, the Mighty Ducks. In 1995, Disney World added an LPGA tour event to its annual PGA championship and acquired the 24-hour ESPN sports cable network as part of its huge deal for ABC/Capital Cities. In January 1996, 50,000 fans watched the Indy Racing

League's first Indy 200 race on Disney's 6-million-dollar one-mile oval track just west of the Magic Kingdom's parking lot; in the same year, they paid an estimated $140 million for the American League's California Angels and $70 million toward the renovation of Anaheim Stadium.

In May 1997, Walt Disney World will unveil a 100-million-dollar sports complex that will be the training camp and pre-season home to the Atlanta Braves, headquarters of the Amateur Athletic Union (AAU) and perennial basketball faves the Harlem Globetrotters, and the greatest permanent center for amateur athletics in the country. Disney knows TV, and even more important, Disney knows audience share. The Boardwalk Resort has its own super sports bar saluting the ESPN sports cable channel and don't forget: Disney also owns the sports-friendly ABC network.

All this bears the mark of Eisner's own interests, just as the Magic Kingdom bears Walt's. Throughout his career, Eisner kept Saturday mornings free to watch his sons' soccer or Little League or football games. Eisner has been to the Indy 500 (that's where he discovered how popular Jim Varney's character "Ernest" was; after returning, he commissioned *Ernest Saves Christmas*). Eisner plays golf. His 1996 summer vacation included a weeklong bicycling trip through the Loire Valley of France. Walt Disney World is now Michael Eisner's park for children of all ages—the children of all ages, '90s style.

• Adult Fare •

The heavier emphasis on young adults is obvious in the food and beverage services, to use corporate biz-speak. After years of sticking to Walt's no-alcohol rule—the one that kept Walt Disney World out of St. Louis—Eisner's Disney World has relaxed it everywhere except within the Magic Kingdom itself. Beer is on sale even on the "street" at EPCOT, where you can drink as you promenade as if you were in New Orleans. The beers even match the national themes: Harp is on tap at the Rose & Crown Pub in the United Kingdom, Dos Equis on draft in Mexico's Cantina de San Angel, Beck's in the German Biergarten, Molson in the Canadian Refreshment Port, Kirin at the Japanese Matsu No Ma, Samuel Adams at *The American Adventure*. Pleasure Island has walk-up bars as well, and there are shops at Disney Village Marketplace and in several of the resort hotel lobbies that have wines and liquor miniatures for retail sale.

Walt Disney World has even jumped on the micro-brewery bandwagon, with custom-brewed house labels at the Territory Lounge in Wilderness Lodge, Outer Rim at the Contemporary, and Harry's Safari Bar at the Dolphin. The Crew's Cup Lounge at the Yacht Club has 36 beers; the Laughing Kookabura at the Buena Vista Palace has 99. The new Boardwalk resort even has its own brewpub, the Big River Grille & Brewworks, with five recipes brewed on the spot.

The fancier restaurants all have long wine lists, and several have special tasting menus as well. Victoria & Albert's in the Grand Floridian has a four-glass flight available for $25; Martha's Vineyard Lounge at the Beach Club, like the big wine bars in New York and Los Angeles, offers almost any of its wines in two-ounce samples. At Arthur's 27 restaurant in the Buena Vista Palace, the private dining room, which holds up to 12 people, is really the wine "cellar," with 800 bottles on display. The California Grill has a very smart all-domestic wine list and a free wine-advice service; call any time between noon and 10 P.M. (phone (407) 824-1576). And, in a bow to new Southwest chic, Only's Bar in the Dolphin stocks a list of rare and aged tequilas.

Other recent consumer trends taken note of are espresso bars (including the Starring Rolls Bakery at MGM and the Fountain View at EPCOT); the exhibition "chef's table" where one party can watch the action up-close (Sum Chows); high tea (Rose & Crown, Grand Floridian's Garden View Lounge); and wood-fired pizza ovens (Palio in the Swan, the California Grill atop the Contemporary Resort, Mama Melrose's at MGM, Portobello at Pleasure Island).

Disney has also taken to contracting with big-name chefs or franchising trendy restaurants with demonstrated market appeal. Paul Bocuse, among others, is touted as having worked on the menu for the Chefs de France and Bistro de Paris in EPCOT. California cuisine star Wolfgang Puck will open a café under his own name when the huge Disney Village Marketplace expansion is finished in 1997; a super-trendy Rainforest Café has already replaced Chef Mickey's there. The Village will also include two celebrity-connected restaurant-nightclubs: the House of Blues, a New Orleans–style nightspot partly owned by surviving Blues Brother, Dan Ackroyd; and Lario's, a Cuban-flavored café created by Gloria Estefan and her husband. There is already a Planet Hollywood at Pleasure Island and, since this one really looks like a planet, it becomes the "globe" entrance that matches EPCOT's Spaceship Earth. And basketball superstar Shaquille O'Neal (who, it should be remembered, starred as the genial genie in Disney's *Kazaam!*) is a celebrity partner in the planned All-Star Sports Café.

Another bit of uptrending is the availability (and more obvious advertising) of "healthy" foods and special-requirement menus. With 24-hours' advance notice, you can have low-sodium, lactose-free, kosher, vegetarian, or vegan meals at many of the restaurants.

But by and large, the new-look kitchens are just that: for looks. The official Birnbaum guide to Walt Disney World describes restaurants as "delicious," "delectable," or "delightful"—it's practically a George Gershwin song. The truth is, little of the food is first-rate. Most of the "serious" ethnic restaurants are uneven in quality. The Teppanyaki Dining Room in the Japan Pavilion at EPCOT specializes in a particularly Westernized form of Japanese cuisine, first produced in New York only about 30 years ago. The Nine Dragons restaurant in the China Pavilion is nearly notorious for its cornstarch-heavy sauces; the eggroll cart at Adventureland is no worse. The only places the culinary staff actually recommend (off the record) are the classic-continental *prix fixe* Victoria & Albert's— where you pay $80 a head to have every waitress introduce herself as Vicky and all the waiters as Al—and the modern-American California Grill, which has one of the only seven ultra-chic Tom Shandley soufflé ovens in the United States.

The simple reason is that gourmets, unlike Super Bowl or NBA stars, are *not* going to Disney World on vacation (or at least, not as a first choice). If the average guest at Walt Disney World were primarily concerned with pleasing his palate, the hottest dinner ticket at the park would not be the *Hoop-Dee-Doo Revue.* So the quality of the food is beside the point, although the standards for purchasing, food storage, and preparation are extremely high. The restaurants, like the rest of Walt Disney World, are sets, part of the nonstop entertainment, either offering costumed servers (at the various World Showcase eateries), live entertainment (the 6,000 sea creatures who swim round and round the glass wall of the Coral Reef), or audio-animatronic distractions (like the Garden Grill, which revolves itself so that the apparent landscape evolves from farmhouse to rain forest to prairie). Even Planet Hollywood, which has a restaurant existence outside of Walt Disney World, is a sort of memorabilia exhibit with fettucini alfredo. Still, even it seems

somewhat theatrical: Hasn't anybody else ever won-
dered what the star partners of Planet Hollywood—
Demi Moore, Bruce Willis, Arnold Schwarzenegger,
Don Johnson, and Sylvester Stallone, all of whose
bodies are insured for millions—actually eat off that
high-calorie menu?

• Pleasure Island •

In the Magic Kingdom, every day is Independence
Day. At Pleasure Island, every night is New Year's Eve.

Pleasure Island is the most specifically adult theme
park within Disney World, with the Boardwalk a close
second. Just as Typhoon Lagoon was built to drain off
the market from Wet 'n' Wild and MGM threatened
to overshadow Universal Studios (and just as the Animal Kingdom will undoubtedly keep more visitors
from venturing to Busch Gardens), Pleasure Island,
which opened in 1989, was inspired by the nightly
traffic at Orlando's downtown club district, Church
Street Station.

One admission ($18) covers the entire complex of
seven nightclubs, as well as assorted restaurants and
souvenir shops. Adults wear a plastic block-party
bracelet that serves as an over-21 ID; those without
the bracelet don't get served at all. Under-21s are
admitted everywhere except Mannequins disco, where
the state-of-the-technopop lighting effects, rotating
dance floor, occasional pro-dancer outbursts, and
shifting mix-and-match crowd make it hard to mon-

itor who's drinking what. There was an all-ages, MTV-style video club when the park first opened. However, since the real money is in liquor, and the majority of the patrons, whether in-towners or park guests, are adults, the club quickly disappeared.

The music on Pleasure Island is safely radio-tested middle-of-the-road. The Neon Armadillo is a C&W saloon that offers potent singles bar–style drinks and free line-dance lessons on Sundays. The music at 8TRAX is mostly '70s golden oldies, leaning heavily toward the retro-kitsch pop and disco. The Rock & Roll Beach Club is also retro, but more classic rock and pop (yeah, surf music); it's mixed live and recorded. The other classic-rock arena is the outdoor West End Stage that treats the street as a club. Its bands tend toward, you guessed it, classic rock. In other words, the music at Pleasure Island is about as segmented as FM oldies programming.

There is an exception—the Pleasure Island Jazz Company—which has some really nice blues and jazz and even the occasional jam, but you wouldn't exactly call it avant-garde.

The seventh club is the most theme-parkish in terms of theatrical experience. In fact, a lot of people find it the only Disneyish place on the island, and it hearkens back to that old obsession of Walt's, the daring derring-doers. The Adventurers Club is a tribute to the swaggering explorers of the late 19th and early 20th centuries, half old-London men's club and half Ripley's Believe-It-or-Not! trophy room. It's a little like a drinking man's Haunted Mansion: shrunken heads, sonorous butlers, macabre-comic souvenir cases, and photos of "members." Invisible ghostly hands play the piano in the library bar, and a rather tawdry music-hall "gypsy" heads up a little vaudeville revue. There are costumed cast members wandering through the club, inducting new members into the secret handshake and the members' special greeting, "Kungaloosh!" The jokes here can be rather subtle, like the giant pharaoh's head that makes up one of the "stone" walls of the entrance (remember all those mummy's curses about entering tombs?); or cartoonish, like the casting rod in the hands of the Poseidon.

Every night Pleasure Island, like the Magic Kingdom, EPCOT, and MGM Studios, sends up a lavish fireworks display; here it's part of a nightly New Year's Eve block party, complete with "Auld Lang Syne." Last call and show time are about 1:30 A.M., and the gates close at 2:00. And just to emphasize the fact that Disney is back in the movie business, the 10-screen cinema by the Pleasure Island entrance, equipped with the George Lucas–designed THX supersound system, is expanding to 24 screens. Plans also call for a 1,500-seat concert hall and performing arts theater to be constructed nearby.

The Boardwalk, which opened in the summer of 1996, is a somewhat more sophisticated nightlife strip, or at least in theory. Themed to the Atlantic City/Long Island resorts of the '30s, it features a dueling-pianos jazz bar called Jelly Roll's; a big band dance club with open-air dancing and a mirror ball; a specialty seafood restaurant; and a trendy-fare Mediterranean al fresco trattoria. The 18-hole miniature golf course, called Fantasia Gardens, also has an exec's-night-out par-3 and par-4 putting course, full of extravagant sand traps and contours.

The Boardwalk also contributes to Disney's elaborate luring of the couch-potato/armchair-quarterback audience with the frenetic ESPN World, a Sportscenter bar with maxi-screen TVs (and a 220-seat "den" to watch them in), 8 Internet hookups, a real broadcasting radio station, constantly updated scores and odds, interactive games, and virtual-reality pods. Hate to break away from the game for essential personal time? Don't worry; there are 14 TV monitors in the rest rooms.

• Prime Playgrounds •

Baseball may have been the all-American pastime when Walt was alive—and amateur sports were followed with affection and respect—but in the quarter-century since Walt Disney World was plotted, sports have become a veritable addiction among Americans. The only question is, is it live or is it Memorex? Are you a spectator or a participant? A physical fitness freak, weekend jock, cable channel-surfing champ, swimsuit contestant, duffer, or driller?

Don't worry. There's something for all categories here, and all carefully tailored for maximum fit and fun. You can book a two-hour bass fishing cruise on Bay Lake, which was originally stocked with 70,000 largemouth bass who've been cheerfully spawning ever since, or you can hang out and stick your cane pole into the equally well-stocked catfish "fishin' hole" at Dixie Landings. Not only can you get tennis lessons, you can play all night on the 24-hour lighted courts at the Dolphin, on clay courts at the Grand Floridian or Disney Institute, or on the ultra-state-of-the-art artificial surfaces in the Racquet Club (hydro-grid clay with buried irrigation). You can even get golf lessons from Gary Player's son Wayne and play any of five courses geared to your proficiency level. (If your handicap is your entire game, try the Lake Buena Vista course.) Or if your drives are really short, you can settle for a game at the two *Fantasia*-themed 18-hole miniature golf courses (a sort of spectator sport with legs).

If you're more serious, of course, four of the five par-72 courses are recommended by *Golf Digest,* and the Osprey Ridge course has a slope rating of 135—as stiff as those at the TPC Stadium in Ponte Vedra. For tour hounds, there's the Walt Disney World/Oldsmobile PGA Classic, which teed off almost as soon as the park opened 25 years ago. (Jack Nicklaus won the first one.) With the boom in women's golf, Disney World has finally addressed the LPGA tee, too; it now hosts the HealthSouth Inaugural, the tour season opener, every January.

Among the newer crazes are croquet (courts at Port

Orleans and the Boardwalk Resort), rock-climbing (classes at the Disney Institute), and parasailing (the Contemporary marina). The three water parks—the small and sweet River Country baby bear, the mixed smooth- and surf-water Typhoon Lagoon, and the 66-acre papa bear, Blizzard Beach—aren't sporting arenas, exactly, although the idea of "skiing" barefooted at 60 miles an hour down 120 feet of water may constitute the thrill of victory and the agony of the feet. You can even scuba dive in The Living Seas if you sign up for the new DiveQuest behind-the-scenes tour (see more below).

But you ain't seen nothin' yet. In 1997, Disney will unveil the 200-acre International Sports Complex, a virtual Olympic development from the designer of Oriole Park at Camden Yards, the Cleveland Indians' Jacobs Field, and the Ballpark at Arlington (Texas). The 100-million-dollar complex will include a 7,500-seat baseball stadium where the Atlanta Braves will play their home exhibition season games, plus four major-league practice fields, 20 major-league pitcher's mounds, and eight batting tunnels; a 5,000-seat fieldhouse with six basketball courts and a track and field complex; four football and soccer playing fields; 12 tennis courts with a 2,000-seat stadium center court; five outdoor sand volleyball courts; and four softball fields; plus the Shaq Shack sports bar. More than 25 AAU championships will be played there the first year, and double that by the end of the decade—half of all AAU title events.

All this may tie into another obvious adult trend in Disney development: the body biz. Most of the hotels already have health clubs—the one at the Dolphin is even the name-brand Body by Jake Health Studio—and several have personal trainers and massage therapists available. It's hard to imagine that the company won't look to draw serious competitors, and even dedicated amateur jocks, to special training camps or seminars.

Then there's the luxury spa industry that is also booming. Many of the newer resorts have whirlpools in addition to the swimming pools; all except the studio apartments at the Disney Vacation Club have whirlpool baths, and the "lighthouse" there doubles as a sauna. There are mud masks, facials, and body scrubs, and classes in low-fat and vegetarian cooking. What would be surprising about a Disney version of the Golden Door?

• High-Class Fun •

Disney CEO Michael Eisner was reportedly inspired to create the Disney Institute when he visited Chatauqua, a small New York town whose series of educational and cultural events, provided for the personal edification of its residents, became the basis of a sort of informal annual tour in the late 19th century. He has also admired the Elderhostel system of offering inexpensive educational vacations for senior citizens at colleges and universities worldwide.

The Institute, which opened in early 1996, has classes in what you might call home studies (a variety of culinary classes, organic gardening and hydroponics, topiary, interior design, gift-making), performing arts (storytelling, improvisation, script writing), media studies (radio deejaying or reporting), sports and health, and even Disney specialties such as animation, coloring, and sound mixing. Altogether there are some 80 workshops. Most are two hours long so that it's possible to take two or even three a day. There are two major performing arts venues there: an outdoor amphitheater that hosts dance troupes, acting companies, and musical concerts; and an indoor recital hall. Institute residents can start the morning with nature walks and t'ai chi sessions; major speakers and artists from all disciplines—Eugenia Zukerman, Pilobolus, Henry Louis Gates, Jr.—appear at night after "classes" are over.

Generally, Institute guests stay three or four days, although there are weeklong packages and even special day services for Florida residents. Four months into its existence, there were not only repeat customers but a few who were on their third visit. Expansion plans are already well underway.

A number of behind-the-scenes tours and educational seminars are conducted around the various theme parks, such as those that let guests in on the customs, taboos, and architectural references in EPCOT's World Showcase (Hidden Treasures and Disney by Design) or landscaping (Planting Ideas,

Gardens of the World); film and animation (Inside Animation and Art Magic); or the machinery behind the magic (Innovation in Action, Backstage Magic, and Keys to the Kingdom).

There are also tours that involve the real world: Wildlife Adventure: Exploring the Environment focuses on the ecosystem of a cypress swamp; Accent on the Environment covers World ecological planning; and EPCOT's D.E.E.P. tour is short for Dolphin Exploration and Education Program, in which participants become guest researchers in actual studies.

• "I Do, I Do," Disney-style •

Finally, there's the romance angle. Not only does Disney design (and promote) certain resorts for singles and young couples, they have expanded their roster of services to include weddings. Big weddings. The $50,000 kind. The mere idea may spell Fantasyland for some budget-conscious fathers, but a surprising number of brides apparently have grown up longing for lavish displays of long-gone romance—and what could be more ornate than Cinderella's own carriage and castle? As a matter of romantic fact, Walt Disney World is now the number one honeymoon destination in the country, and two or three couples exchange their actual vows there every day.

There are dedicated wedding coordinators who spend six or eight months getting every detail arranged, from the procession to the pixie dust. The most elaborate weddings take place in the Magic Kingdom: The groom rides in on a white horse (led by a lawsuit-savvy attendant); followed by the guests in open touring cars or trolleys; and the bride herself in a fair imitation of a crystal coach, with eight miniature horses small enough to have been white mice in a previous life. The wedding is staged—usually after hours—in the rose garden below Cinderella Castle, and for an additional $15,000 or so, another fireworks display can be thrown in instead of mere rice. (Yes, and pixie dust, too.)

There is a garden gazebo at the Yacht Club that is popular, but in 1995 Disney opened the larger Fairy Tale Wedding pavilion: a truly elaborate glass-sided Victorian gazebo on its own little island near the Grand Floridian, that also looks up at Cinderella Castle. Of course, most of the hotels have lavish honeymoon suites if you want to cut to the chase.

But don't start your honeymoon in the Magic Kingdom. For some reason, it never seems to occur to couples that even the darkest tunnels and rides in Walt Disney World have to be monitored for safety reasons, and that means some of your "private time" may not be as private as you expect.

Pirates of the Caribbean is a popular site for amorous couples who think they can't be seen and wind up giving monitor-watchers an X-rated show. Cast members assigned to Space Mountain have reported finding "slightly used panties, but no bras." On the other hand, lifeguards prize being assigned to flume duty at River Country and Blizzard Beach, where two-piece bathing suits are fairly frequently reduced to one piece. And there was a flurry of publicity concerning an Internet video of women lifting their T-shirts while riding down Splash Mountain. Although it was later argued that the film came from Disneyland, the fact that there was any confusion about the source is just as, well, revealing.

AMERICA'S ADVENTURES IN WONDERLAND

The Disney Version of History

The Magic Kingdom represents Walt Disney's idealized view of his childhood, his creative philosophy, and his most devoted principles. Most of all, it is Disney's paean to America: the Greatest Nation on Earth, produced as the Greatest Show on Earth.

But the Magic Kingdom is also in some ways Disney World's most troubling theme park, because it presents a view of American history that leaves out more Americans than it includes. Disney World's version of American history is technologically the most advanced you'll ever see, but sociologically and politically, it's decades out of date.

H. L. Mencken said that the power of the press belongs to the man who owns one; it is just as true that history is at the service of the historian who writes it. Disney, as pointed out in "The World According to Walt," saw the country in terms of the discoveries and the leaps of imagination that opened physical and industrial frontiers. Those were primarily the accomplishments of white Anglo-American males. That those same advances had negative impacts on blacks, women, Native Americans, or immigrants meant little to Disney, or to the majority of Americans in the first half of the 20th century.

But *The American Adventure* was renovated in 1993. Walt Disney World's Splash Mountain, built in 1992, takes its Uncle Remus characters from *Song of the South,* a 1946 movie whose idyllic antebellum plantation and placid black slaves are not exactly a celebrated bit of political correctness. (The Birnbaum Guide to Walt Disney World says "Zip-A-Dee-Doo-Dah" has become "something of a Disney anthem over the years.") The American history theme park that the Disney Company had hoped to build in the Virginia countryside near Washington, D.C.—the one that would have turned the Underground Railroad into a sort of "slave escape" thrill ride—was conceived in 1994. All this on the watch of CEO Michael Eisner, who once helped launch the ABC-TV series *Roots,* which transformed popular culture in so many ways.

So before we enjoy the nostalgia and the artistry, let's walk through the history. The past, after all, is prologue.

• Main Street, U.S.A. •

The central symbol of Walt Disney's desire to mythologize the past is Main Street, U.S.A., the heart of the

Magic Kingdom. In only slightly disguised form, it is the main artery of the EPCOT and Disney-MGM Studio parks, too. Main Street was so close to Disney's heart that it is the only place in the entire World that you will see his full name written out. Stand at the corner of the ice cream parlor and look up at the wall of the second floor. You'll see, written in gold, the legend "Walter Elias Disney." So it's worth stopping here for a moment to consider its message.

In fact, you *have* to stop here; you cannot avoid it. The Main Street of Walt Disney World is the sole access to the Magic Kingdom. There is no other corridor, intentionally: Walt Disney wanted every person who visited the park to begin by walking the Main drag. It leads to Cinderella Castle and to the other areas of the park. But Main Street is some sort of psychological requirement—the fairy-tale trial. Only after passing this particular facade may visitors enter their own "realm" of the Kingdom.

Main Street is the first glimpse everyone has of the Magic Kingdom. It is also frequently the last vision they have for the night, since Main Street stays open longer than the rest of the Magic Kingdom. It turns unrelated visitors into a crowd, a temporary "community," by gently funneling them in together. (It's only 55 feet wide, half to two-thirds the size of a real street at the turn of the century.) It is the site of regular "town meetings": the afternoon kiddie spectacular, the nightly grand parade and Tinkerbell's flight, and the climactic fireworks above the

Castle turrets. In the Magic Kingdom, every day is the Fourth of July.

But if Main Street is the first stop on Walt's Magical History Tour, it is also the first evidence of the custom-tailored nostalgia that characterizes the park. Disney World's Main Street may have been intended to evoke the Missouri main street of Walt's childhood, but only in the form he decided to remember.

Dirt was an inescapable element of those times: streets of mud and haphazard sidewalks, sawdust floors, spittoons, outhouses, crudely painted signs (and even cruder paintings to accommodate the illiterate), fencing, poles leaning under the weight of layers of wires (for telegraph, telephone, and electricity), horse and cow manure, haphazard window glazing or even open holes. Clouds of tobacco issued from every barbershop, stable, and foodstore, not to mention the tobacconist's. Railway stations reeked of smoke, coal, animal freight, sweat, and dung.

Not this one. If cleanliness is next to godliness, Walt Disney World is the closest thing to heaven. Walt Disney's Main Street is so immaculate that not many children have the chutzpah to drop an ice cream wrapper on the sidewalk. There is a trash can ("Waste Please") every few yards. Chewing gum isn't even sold in Walt Disney World, just to limit the amount of the gunk that has to be removed. The paint is constantly refreshed—the horse-shaped iron hitching posts are scraped entirely clean and repainted twice a month—and the architectural trim and details are made of fiberglass rather than wood; no fading or weather-beating is allowed. Brass glitters and glass gleams. Even the false second-floor windows open into rooms only about three feet deep which are carefully wall-papered and painted. Every fixture and piece of furniture is correct to the period.

This is no financially marginal Midwest farm town, but an old and moneyed community. The shops are obviously prosperous, and the square has not one but two "public greens." This is no place on Earth, much less turn-of-the-century rural America. It's Main Street to the max, with more columns, more gingerbread, more flowers, and more commodities than could ever have been found in one place.

All the jobs are "respectable"—no amenable saloon girls or pickpockets or quacks or con men. (And no castoff Chinese laborers.) There are no pool parlors or prisons, in Disney's America; no doctor's office, no hospital, and certainly no funeral parlor. No school and, more surprisingly, no church. Barbers sing as well as snip. The horses that draw the trolleys would seem to have evolved beyond the usual digestive functions; any unfortunate manure that is exuded is barely allowed to land before being collected by street sweepers. In fact, except for Walt's own finickiness about such excretory things, you'd say Main Street was the embodiment of "spit and polish" decor. In Walt Disney's America, equal opportunity is not enough—equal prosperity and equal hygiene are also guaranteed.

Even before the fireworks you get the holiday atmosphere. The music you hear recalls outdoor picnics and town fairs: brass bands, barbershop quartets, player pianos. The air is redolent of popcorn, cotton candy, and just-baked cookies. The sidewalks are straight and the promenades inviting. (The "pavement" is a special slightly resilient asphalt blend, painted to resemble paving but designed to be easier on the feet.) The Crystal Palace, modeled on the showcase of one of those great expositions, the London Exhibition of 1851, sets out a banquet so lavish it would have fed the entire population of several such Midwestern towns.

There are evocations of several primary American myths, from the Founding Fathers and nascent democracy (City Hall and the volunteer fire department), to the democratization of "culture" (a theater and even an opera house); and from the boom-days bank (a working SunTrust branch), to an idyllic and pre-inflationary childhood (a candy store—Walt's personal retreat—and an ice cream parlor). And above it all is the railroad depot.

The railroad, of course, represents one of Walt Disney's favorite Great American Myths—the binding up of a continent and the "taming" of the Wild West—as well as his own first bit of personal conceit and the birthplace of Mickey himself. Walt had his railway laid all around the perimeter of the Magic Kingdom, had another built into Big Thunder Mountain, and had the monorail, the train of the future, run around the park. In his honor, there is a model railroad in EPCOT's Germany Pavilion. (Walt was a dedicated model railroader.) But the Magic Kingdom station might as well be "Shining Time Station," or the Phantom Tollbooth: The route doesn't run on real time, or on real historical grounds.

• Give Me Liberty Square, or •
Give Me Justice

Liberty Square and Frontierland are laid out along the canal in a way that is both "geographical"—from the Atlantic to the Pacific—and "chronological," following the westward expansion of the country. The Haunted Mansion at the top corner of Liberty Square is a Dutch New Amsterdam showplace. Therefore, the river it overlooks is presumably the Hudson River. The water skims New England, passing the Boston/Philly town square and the Yankee Trader complex and becomes the Erie Canal and the Ohio River (depending on which keelboat pilot you get). Where Davy Crockett's canoes pass, it suggests the great Tennessee and Cumberland rivers and then becomes the Mississippi, where the Mark Twain paddle wheeler cruises to Tom Sawyer Island. Beyond that point, in Frontierland, the river might be the Missouri (the Diamond Horseshoe Saloon) or perhaps the Colorado. Whichever it is, it finally lands you in California just in time for the Gold Rush (Big Thunder Mountain). The various waters of Adventureland, which manage to mingle the rivers of at least three continents, are almost generic—foreign.

Symbolically speaking, Liberty Square is the oldest part of Disney's America. However, it only goes back to the British era, and not even the very beginning of that, skipping John Smith (and Pocahantas), Walter Raleigh, and the first Thanksgiving (and Squanto). America is already established and mercantile when Walt drops in. The architecture of the main buildings of Liberty Square is Federal (Boston, Philadelphia) and Georgian (Williamsburg). The shops have clapboard siding or brick walls, white porticos, and neat signs of "ye olde shoppe" nostalgia. The centerpieces of this park are the Liberty Tree Tavern, where costumed patriots occasionally rail against the King's taxes, the Liberty Tree, and *The Hall of Presidents,* whose audio-animatronic Chief Executives are one of Disney's most popular attractions.

The first audio-animatronic "human" to debut was Abraham Lincoln—a Midwesterner, and a man whose physiognomy was so familiar, and whose reputation was so solid, that they made him a safe bet to win over the audience. He was the star of the 1964 World's Fair and remains a figurehead for Disney wizardry. Although he no longer talks for as long as he once did, he is still seated at the front of the stage, in prominent view at all times. He is also important as a symbol of civil rights, and, oy, there's the rub.

On the surface, the Clinton-era version of *The Hall of Presidents* show is more politically correct, as far as black Americans are concerned, than its previous scripts. Poet Maya Angelou, who, not coincidentally, wrote the official poem for Clinton's 1993 inauguration, has taken over the narrator's role. Her voice is full and rousing. She speaks of dreams of freedom and national dedication, and the implication of her presence is that this great struggle for liberty has succeeded. But in re-editing the script to give civil rights priority, the Disney writers have exposed an equally clumsy willingness to try to make it all okay—and then make it all go away.

The first scene portrays the delegates of the First Continental Congress wrangling over the wording of the Declaration of Independence. The southern representatives, so this version goes, are fighting solely to have the peculiar institution of slavery protected in the document. It takes the combined eloquence of Benjamin Franklin and George Washington to get the paper signed.

The next great icon of Disney history to appear is Andrew Jackson, whose near-savage treatment of rebellious Seminoles and Creeks and whose personal slave-owning are never mentioned. On the contrary, Jackson's famous devotion to the Union is portrayed not as pro-federalism but as anti-slavery. "If one drop of blood is shed . . . I will hang the first man of them I can get my hands on."

From there we jump to the Lincoln–Douglas debates, featuring that ringing phrase, "all men are created equal." If that premise is not true, Lincoln tells the restive crowd, then they'd better dismantle the entire sacred document. His audience—including what must be the most passive Indian in Illinois—is immediately roused to defend the Declaration. Nevertheless, the narrator points out, Lincoln lost that election, by implication because of his pro-emancipation stance.

But only a couple of years later, things have changed. Lincoln is in the White House and aging rapidly in the face of the gathering storm. Sketches of soldiers, all white: "Soon the blood of our nation was shed in a great Civil War," Angelou intones. "And when it was over . . . ." That's it. *That's it* for the crucial conflict that, according to this very same show, all of American history had been leading up to. Almost immediately we cut to a picture of the glowing Capitol dome at night—a picture that resembles nothing so much as that modern cultural touchstone, the nighttime talk show backdrop.

Now the curtain rises on the parade of presidents. From Washington to Clinton, each one is spotlighted and named by the sonorous Angelou, and each exactly-sized and costumed president acknowledges his introduction by nodding, gesturing, or slightly bowing. The sitting president always has a speaking role, and Clinton's speech is strictly tailored to the Disney script doctors' theory of enlightened American society. Now that "we" have such freedom, Clinton reminds us, "we" must keep fighting to ensure the same rights for those—apparently in other galaxies far, far away—who don't yet have them. This must be reassuring for white middle-class spectators, but some minority visitors must find themselves muttering, "We who, white man?"

Yet, as you walk out of the hall, surrounded by fellow audience members who are, for the most part, looking moved and satisfied, you can't help but realize that Disney's conceptualizers know exactly for whom they script: The percentage of black guests is very low, and those who do come, generally teenagers or twenty-somethings, are not terribly attracted to that sort of entertainment. They're over at *Alien Encounter* and Space Mountain. The ordinary visitor to Disney World wants to believe that the Founding Fathers had only the purest motives for breaking away from Britain: that the leaders of this country—elected, after all, by the right-thinking majority of citizens— were always committed to equal rights, and that somehow it is a reality. We know this because Honest Abe and Uncle Walt just told us so.

• Frontierland: From the Midwest • to the Wild West

As you cross the subtle bridge between Liberty Square and Frontierland, you stroll out of the 18th century and into the 19th, and from the civilized towns of the Northeast into the wilderness. The *Country Bear Jamboree* is in the Rockies somewhere, and the Diamond Horseshoe Saloon is somewhere between Tombstone and San Francisco.

Around here, the Native American, rather than the black American, is the missing link. Tom Sawyer Island is the site of an Army fort—named, in a bit of irony he might not have appreciated, for Tom's open-minded creator, Sam Clemens. The canoes are credited not to their native inventors but to that noted Indian-slayer, Davy Crockett. You can buy a coonskin cap and take aim with a real, restored buffalo rifle in the Frontierland Shootin' Gallery, without ever hearing a peep about how white trophy hunters slaughtered the buffalo out of train windows for sport and left the carcasses to rot (and the Plains Indians to starve).

The only good Indians in the Magic Kingdom are, if not dead, powerless: the women, children, and ceremonially buried corpse in the Indian village on Tom Sawyer Island.

• America's Progressive Adventures •

The same selective editing of the national legend that characterizes the *Hall of Presidents* performance is evident in *The American Adventure*, the newer and in many ways more technologically impressive audio-animatronic show in EPCOT. This America may be broader in constituency, but no deeper. It isn't only black Americans who are subjected to the patronizing rewrite of history here, it's also women, immigrants, and Native Americans. Those few who aren't omitted have been manipulated into serving the Disney script. This is sad, because the two animated hosts in this case are forward-thinkers Mark Twain and Ben Franklin, who begin by debating the progress of the nation.

Here, except for a brief salute to the Founding Fathers, the heroes are those inventors and adventurers who inspired the young Walt Disney himself, only re-interpreted as cultural boosters. Befitting this particular bias, our Fathers (like the rest of EPCOT) have big corporate backing. "And now, on behalf of Coca-Cola, American Express, and the Walt Disney Company," the host says with no trace of embarrassment, "welcome to *The American Adventure!*"

America is still "discovered" by the British (cue the sea chanteys), but it goes back a century further, to the *Mayflower*, and has an extra pure-minded dimension: The first immigrants are looking not for commercial opportunity or land or escape from debt—only religious freedom. It's a tough crossing, of course, for those poor seekers of liberty, at least for the Y-chromosomed ones. (In the picture that goes with this *Mayflower* moment, all the ailing pilgrims are male and all the ministering angels are women.)

Thanksgiving and its native hosts are skipped over again. Once the pilgrims get to Plymouth Rock, they find no friendly Indians and no gifts of corn; in fact, they apparently find no humans at all, only snow and starvation. This is an "untamed" land, just waiting for the right (!) sort of men to whip it into shape, and they go at it with great determination. But soon they quarrel with Mother England and throw the Boston

Tea Party. Mother closes Boston Harbor, and colonists in breeches and powdered wigs gather in fury around the tavern door. Among them is a black, presumably a freeman, and, aside from his complexion, he is indistinguishable from the rest of the wigs. Shortly after that, Franklin "climbs" the stairs into Thomas Jefferson's study and begs him to hurry up with the Declaration of Independence.

Always in a hurry. A quick stop at Valley Forge (which, technically speaking, is the most lifelike of the sequences, thanks to Washington's horse) and we're a nation, spreading across Tennessee and Missouri. Suddenly Twain, the subtle creator of Jim, the runaway slave, rumbles, "It seems a whole bunch of folks found out 'We the people' didn't yet mean all the people"—something most Native and black Americans had known for quite a while.

The second black American, orator Frederick Douglass, comes into animated view, but not, as one might have hoped, in front of a crowd. Douglass, who would probably have been lynched if caught below the Mason-Dixon line, is seen rowing a small boat through the Louisiana bayou. "Even along Mark Twain's beloved Mississippi," Douglass says, "I hear the rattle of chains and the crack of the whip." And this tireless and eloquent agitator credits Harriet Beecher Stowe, the white author of *Uncle Tom's Cabin,* with making the coming Civil War possible.

When it does come, in a sepia montage reminiscent of Ken Burns's immensely successful PBS series, it focuses on a white family divided by politics. A woman sings about "Two Brothers," one of whom dies and fades from the "Matthew Brady" family portrait. War is over, again.

Twain then says something about "the wisdom of Chief Joseph," and the figure of the Nez Percé chief, the sole Native American identified in the entire show, rises into view. But his speech with its famous finale, "I will fight no more forever," is made to sound not like a surrender but like a conversion—an endorsement of the white man's expansionist vision instead of weary recognition of his greater firepower. Everyone, apparently, is eager to become an American.

Chief Joseph is followed by what should be a fun sequence: Twain, Andrew Carnegie, and Alexander Graham Bell ("Ah, the proud Scots!" Twain jokes) at the Philadelphia Centennial Exposition. It also features an audio-animatronic Susan B. Anthony. Yet again, her speech implies that the call for women's equality has not only been heard, but already heeded. There, in 1876. We don't even need to worry about suffrage, much less an equal rights amendment.

Next up is "green" hero John Muir, whose robotic self argues with spraddle-legged Teddy Roosevelt on a peak in Yosemite. They are followed swiftly by film of flyboy heroes Eddie Rickenbacker and Charles Lindbergh (whose pro-Fascist sentiments are, of course, ignored).

Now comes a truly astonishing sequence. It is the Depression. FDR is on the radio, and also in audio-

animatronic person, talking about "fear itself." Will
Rogers twirls a rope at the other side of the stage. And
on the porch of a southern rural gas station sit four
men: two whites and two totally relaxed, familiarly
joking blacks (one strumming a guitar, which is at
least better than a banjo). There's no Ku Klux Klan or
even prejudice to fear in this America. We apparently
never had a race problem, any more than we had sex
discrimination, underprivileged Indians, or any other
minority. Or a gender gap in salary, either—Rosie the
Riveter makes sure of that.

The last half-century spins by in a montage of
photos in no obvious order and with no identifica-
tion. Among them are Judy Garland, Leonard Bern-
stein, Bob Hope, Mary Martin as Peter Pan, Eisenhower, Eleanor Roosevelt, Chief Dan George, Gloria
Steinem, Billie Jean King, Bob Dylan, Alex Haley,
Marilyn Monroe, Johnny Carson, Walt Disney himself, Albert Einstein, Frank Sinatra, Neil Armstrong,
Frank Lloyd Wright, Elvis, JFK, Sally Ride, and Mary
Lou Retton. There is a sound bite from Martin Luther
King, "I have a dream today," but it rushes by.

Finally, a photo of the Statue of Liberty is replaced
by a life-sized torch on which Twain and Franklin are
standing. So what does Twain think of this brash little country? "I think the Founding Fathers never
dreamed of an America like this," says Twain. It may
be the understatement of the century.

The lights come up on the statuary niches along
either side of the stage. And look: the "Spirit of Her-

itage" is what they used to call an Indian maiden, her eyes demurely cast down. One wonders who was around to inherit what.

• Exotic Adventureland •

The politically incorrect elements in Adventureland are at least less concentrated than those in the history pageants, and the Disney Company seems to have eased a few of them out in recent years. However, the Jungle Cruise still smacks of white civilization vs. native primitivism. The spear-waving Africans are straight out of a *Tarzan* film (Edgar Rice Burroughs's classic was published when Walt was 13), and the hired hands, the "native porters" also familiar from B-movies, are stuck supplying the sort of clumsy comic relief that Hollywood long ago abandoned. There is also a little egregious violence and the geographical convenience that the cruise route covers Africa, Southeast Asia, and South America simultaneously. You know—they all look alike.

The condescension of Pirates of the Caribbean, on the other hand, is turned toward women, although the mongrelized pirates themselves aren't exactly attractive. One woman captive, dressed to suggest an already casual attitude toward men, is scolded by her self-appointed auctioneer for "advertising" her physical wares; another is being chased by a drunken pirate through the doors of her home, cheery as a cuckoo-clock hausfrau. An official Walt Disney World picture book says, "While their victims may fret just a bit, they seem to be having as much fun as the buccaneers." In other words, if rape is inevitable, everybody should enjoy it. Disney's major concession to political correctness in the last couple of years has been to eliminate the scene of a fat woman in pursuit of a fat pirate. Score one for the heavyweight lobby.

Pirates of the Caribbean has been around for 20 years, and it's too popular to dismantle. But the condescending mindset doesn't seem to have been dismantled yet, either. In the reception area of the spanking new and generally admirable Disney Institute, several "paintings" purport to illustrate the kinds of adult classes and recreation available for registrants: cooking, aerobics, golf, and gardening. The fashions are vaguely Eisenhower era, and so are the stereotypes. In the kitchen scene, the women are cooking and the men are tasting. In the gym, the man is shown impressively balanced on the rings with his arms straight out at his sides, as perfectly horizontal as a model airplane. The women, on the other hand, are doing "spa" things, like standing in one of those fat-jiggling fanny bands (a scene also enacted in the frequently condescending *Carousel of Progress*). In the photography studio, the cameras are operated by men while the women pose. And so on.

There are black figures in these pictures, but their faces are indistinguishable from the others except for the tinting, and their hair has no noticeable texture.

It's especially true of female characters, including various dolls in It's a Small World and more recently Princess Jasmine and Pocahontas. Maybe it's time Disney discovered the world is wide, after all.

ANIMAL, VEGETABLE, OR MINERAL?

The "Real" World

*R*unning the real-world systems at Walt Disney World may not seem as much fun as maintaining the Magic Kingdom, but it's just as complex a process. Disney World is so huge and varied that it isn't possible even for its agricultural staff to keep a running tally of all the plants, or for its veterinary biologists to be sure how many birds are on-site at any given time. All you have to do is glance around to realize what a huge task grooming the theme park is. But there are a few especially notable examples of Disney's green thumb and its lucky rabbits' feet—places to admire the landscaping and pat the bunny. And daunting as it may sound, the company does know almost exactly how much water there is in the World, how many lights are on, and even how many kilowatt-hours are used. (It's all on computer.)

There is one thing you'll rarely notice about your surroundings: garbage. Disney's waste removal system and recycling programs are also state of the art, and its recycling program is admirable. In 1995, it recycled nearly 1,000 tons of cardboard and 18 tons of steel and aluminum, among other materials.

• It's Not Easy Being Green •

"Poems were made by fools like me," Joyce Kilmer rhapsodized. "But only God can make a Tree."

Joyce Kilmer never met the Imagineers.

At Walt Disney World, trees are not just cultivated, they're, well, made—custom-tailored, cloned, and constantly relocated. Because of the strict visual requirements (taller plants in back, shorter ones in front, skinny ones in limited spaces), trees have to be constantly monitored for size and kept in proportion to the buildings they flank. Therefore, several "stand-ins" are cultivated for each planting, with at least one in the same stage of development as its model, in case the one on view is damaged or blighted somehow, and several other "twins" that are months younger. Replacement or new-character topiaries, those pruned and shaped tree-animals visible in the Magic Kingdom and around the Seven Seas Lagoon, may be several years in the making, so extra care has to be taken to ensure the originals thrive.

When the starring tree gets too big or turns temperamental it is jerked overnight and replaced by one of the understudies before anybody notices. Some are moved to bigger quarters; the four trees in front of

The American Adventure are in their fifth location. The better specimens among these outgrown trees and their discarded replacements are usually resold to area nurseries and often show up in full-grown splendor around Orlando golf courses and luxury homes; the smaller or less valuable ones may be mulched or moved into less visible areas.

Sometimes relocating trees isn't an option. In the case of Cinderella Castle, the plantings could not be allowed to interfere with the underground corridors of the Utilidor, but neither did the Imagineers want gardeners to have to fiddle around with the Castle landscaping, the most visible in the park. So when the complex was being built, huge containers were framed around the "ceiling" of the tunnels and filled with a special mix. Then the root balls of the trees were placed in these permanent containers and maintained by spray hoses of water and nutrients pointed right into their hanging pots.

Sometimes relocation is only half the problem. Birnbaum says the lovely old olive trees in the Italy showcase at EPCOT ran afoul of Arizona wide-load regulations on their way east from California and had to be cut to 10 feet by chain saw. (The older bark is darker, so you can gauge the change.) But they survived to join the other imports.

Actually, Joyce Kilmer probably would have thought he was in heaven if he'd strolled the Walt Disney World grounds. The sheer extravagance of some of the landscapes, either authentic or theatrical, is breathtaking. On Tom Sawyer Island the forest includes sycamores, maples, oaks, pines, firethorn, azalea, Brazilian pepper trees, elms, and holly, among others. Frontierland is shaded by maples, oaks, sycamores, birches, cactus, and pines—an assortment that you'd have to drive several days to see in real life. The Jungle Cruise, which encompasses three continents, combines trees from an even wider world tour—rubber trees, Malaysian tiger grass, bamboo, papyrus, palms, jacarandas, ferns, lianas, orchids—some of which have to be coddled with hot air from gas heaters hidden in the rocks when temperatures drop into the 30s. The Adventureland bridge cradles South African cape honeysuckle, Chinese hibiscus, Australian tree ferns, Mexican flame vines, Brazilian bougainvillea, and dime-store spider plants. The three-story atrium of the Polynesian Resort is a huge garden with its own waterfall that keeps the air moist enough to suit even the tropically-minded anthuria, gardenias, orchids, and coconut palms.

There are already 3,500 acres of landscaping in Walt Disney World, requiring about 40,000 trees and a half-million shrubs. Before the opening of the Animal Kingdom in 1998, Disney landscapers will have to transplant and nourish another 30,000 or so live trees, suitable for African and Asian animal life, on the 500-acre site.

Transplanting isn't always so simple, however, as is suggested by the story of Liberty Square's Liberty Oak Tree. The 100-year-old Southern live oak, *Quercus vir-*

giniana, which evokes the Liberty Tree in Boston under which the Sons of Liberty gathered, was discovered on park territory, but a good six miles from its current home in the Magic Kingdom. At 40 feet tall, with a canopy 60 feet across, and at an estimated 135 years of age, it was much too large just to be dolleyed free or roped and lifted out—the root ball was four feet across—so steel rods were screwed into the hardwood and used as hooks to haul it free with a huge crane. Once it was replanted, the rods were removed and the wood plugs that had been drawn out were replaced. Guidebooks say that nowadays, the tree looks right at home, "as if it had been growing happily in Liberty Square since the Revolution." But as Birnbaum reveals, it wasn't quite that simple. The wood plugs became contaminated; the tree became infected; and a large section of the interior rotted. The plugs had to be pulled out again, the rotted sections vacuumed, and the holes filled with cement. A younger, presumably virgin *virginiana*, was grafted into the base, where you can easily see it if you know what to look for.

There are two other less striking examples of this massive repotting. One is at the entrance to EPCOT: a massive three-trunk palm that had to be amputated into its three parts and then rejoined on the site. And when the Boardwalk villas were being constructed, Disney engineers rescued a huge specimen that clearly had a future on display. But, because there wasn't anyplace to put it, it spent several weeks in a temporary holding pen—the swimming pool.

There is also one tree that seems to have taken its destiny into its own roots, rather than accept the Disney plan. The so-called Lawnmower Tree at Fort Wilderness, just off the marina path, either took revenge on an errant mower or gradually expanded around a forgotten one in hopes of hiding it.

But since the niggling details of real life—pruning, fertilizing, root trimming—are to be kept out of sight, not performed in public, Disney World often uses artificial plants in the seemingly liveliest places. All the trees in view on the Living with the Land ride in EPCOT, which ranges through prairie, deserts, and rain forest scenes, are also plastic, except those in the greenhouses. The most impressive one in the whole Land, the sycamore outside the farmhouse, is a molded-and-cast copy of one at a carwash near Disneyland.

Starting from Scratch

Like almost everything else, the landscaping at Walt Disney World is sketched out on the Imagineers' storyboards and then the plants are grown to suit. Disney World's main tree farm covers 120 acres, and the saplings serve double duty as water filters. Some of the less polluted waste water is used to irrigate the trees, whose roots extract some chemical nutrients and reject others.

In the greenhouses at The Land, however, an even more high-tech nursery is at least partly visible. Endangered species of trees, especially those that were once native to the central Florida sand ridge, are being cloned for transplanting to the Disney Wilderness Preserve. A large number of the plants used for cloning experiments at Walt Disney World (including those test tube–sized samples laid out for viewing by visitors who take the behind-the-scenes tours) are bear grass, scrub palm, and silkbay—all plants that were indigenous to the Florida sand ridge. A refrigerator-like vault with controlled humidity, light, and temperature dominates the room, and a photo collage, similar to an elementary school exhibit, shows botanists and Nature Conservancy volunteers planting these specimens back at the preserve. These test-tube baby trees are also available at the souvenir stands.

(It must have seemed a sad sort of joke to the Imagineers when the Nature Conservancy overseers of the Disney Wilderness Preserve decided that the trees there didn't "look right" to the putative residents, and would have to come down. In order to restore the wetlands and attract wildlife, stands of long-leaf pines had to be clear cut, and other areas of palmetto and shrub had to be control-burned.)

Trees and shrubs are not the only green genes in this show. Disney is deeply involved in growing food and shelter crops in experimental ways: hydroponic and air-grown, genetically-engineered, and in "closed-system" cultures that speed up natural growing processes. Drought- and disease-resistant varieties, vertically trained vegetables vines, and organically fertilized fruits are displayed, along with the cloned specimens and environmentally friendly species, such as the naturally blue cotton strain that will eliminate the need to dye denim for jeans. Many of the experiments are supported by grants from NASA and the U.S. Department of Agriculture, and, like all the pavilions at EPCOT, The Land has major corporate sponsorship, in this case from Kraft Foods.

This takes a little of a bloom off the program. As has been pointed out by other critics, Disney never addresses the cost of building and maintaining such facilities in Third World countries, which are nominally the intended beneficiaries of these agricultural advances. Such programs could just as easily be seen as capitalism rather than altruism: ways of providing more commodities, or more commercial construction contracts, for the developed world to sell to less prosperous economies. Why not simply persuade the inhabitants of poorer nations to wear something other than jeans in imitation of American yuppies?

• "I Went to the Animal Fair . . ." •

"Animals" is an interesting concept in Walt Disney World, where the most famous characters tend to have tails. Disney's animated characters are more folk than fauna, with voices and vocabularies (in the movies, at least) and emotions large and small. They are half-creatures, metaphorical versions of the centaurs of *Fantasia* or the Little Mermaid herself.

The full-length animated features, the ones with

fairy-tale heroes and witches like *Cinderella* or *Snow White,* tend to mix and match cartoon mice and "real" horses: The Cheshire Cat and the White Rabbit are cartoons; Thumper, Bambi, and all 101 dalmatians are real; Jiminy Cricket is a cartoon, while the dragon in *Sleeping Beauty* is very real indeed. The real-life films, of course, use long-range lenses and natural settings with no animated characters at all. Once it opens, the 500-acre Animal Kingdom will cover all the bases, with animals that are alive, animated, animatronic, and imaginary (see below).

Most of the live animals at Walt Disney World have been kept in very limited roles, so to speak. There was Grandma Duck's Petting Farm in the Magic Kingdom and another petting zoo at Fort Wilderness. Draft horses pull the trolleys down Main Street (check the bridle hardware for Hidden Mickeys), and special miniature white horses are on call for bridal carriage duty.

There have also been some unexpected appearances by alligators and snakes, as well as the less disturbing rabbits, ducks, squirrels, and mice, on Tom Sawyer Island. Cast members say the island's opening had to be delayed one day when a pair of alligators discovered what a good sunning spot the main deck was. Staffers joke that these periodic invasions are failed character auditions: "Critters can stay only if they present you with a valid World passport," meaning a Disney I.D. The only animals allowed in from the outside are seeing- or hearing-guide dogs. All others must be

lodged in one of the Pet Care Kennels, and it's a tes-
tament to the handlers' aplomb that they've been left
in charge of ocelots, cougars, and even bears, as well
as various snakes, rabbits, and exotic novelties.

But by and large, the live animals are left to act naturally in and around the resorts, the undeveloped
areas, and on Discovery Island. Golfers have reported
seeing deer, otters, turkeys, bald eagles, and even some
big cats, panthers, and bobcats. Even outside the petting zoos, just on the lawns of the resorts, there are
animals so tame they feed out of guests' hands; squirrels, egrets, and ducks have all been spotted partaking
of doughnuts.

Discovery Island may look as though it's a rare "natural" bit of Walt Disney World, but it's another Imagineering triumph: It was just a scrub beach before the
hauling over of a few million pounds of exotic landscaping and a shipwreck and christened Treasure
Island. (The name is gone, but the ship lists on.) Now
a tropical paradise, its 11 acres are home to more than
100 species of birds and animals that, in typical Disney fashion, would ordinarily be continents apart:
giant Galapagos tortoises, an Indian fishing cat, bald
eagles (who are not, it seems, very collegial), ospreys,
alligators, swallowtail kites, red-cockaded wood-
peckers, trumpeter swans, Asian muntjac deer, pea-
cocks, rabbit-like Patagonian cavies, and various small
primates.

Its emphasis is on birdlife, and two of its presen-
tations, *Feathered Friends* and *Birds of Prey,* showcase

the tropical species such as rose cockatoos and hyacinth macaws; the endangered toco toucans and brown pelicans; and predators such as hawks, vultures, and owls. Discovery Island is accredited by the American Association of Zoological Parks and Aquariums, and is the site of one of the most successful breeding programs for flamingos and scarlet ibis in the world. In 1983, it launched a last-ditch campaign to save the last four dusky sparrows living there by mating them with mixed Scott-dusky sparrows, but unfortunately the effort failed. It has a veterinary hospice for injured animals—you can observe the staff through large windows—and a wild-release training center there.

Discovery Island was also the site of Disney's most egregious act of cruelty. In 1989, battling vultures that were attacking the animals on the island, stealing their food, and defecating on the boardwalk—a potential health hazard to humans—Disney employees captured some vultures and caged them in a small overheated shed; beat others to death; and, in cases of wildly mistaken identity (or guilt by association), shot hawks and falcons and destroyed the eggs in egret and ibis nests. Federal and state officials filed 16 charges against the company, but rather than endure a public court case, Disney agreed to pay a total of $95,000— three times what it would have been fined if it had been convicted of all 16 charges.

Disney Wilderness Preserve:
The Great Land Swap

During the original planning for Walt Disney World, the ecological engineers found a half-dozen different ecosystems, including a 7,500-acre cypress swamp that is now a wildlife refuge and the site of in-depth studies of plant groupings, symbiotic ecosettings, and water management. "Ninety percent of the scrub habitat has been lost to agriculture and urbanization," says one agricultural botanist at The Land, without necessarily pointing out that Disney has been the region's largest developer. But without actually calling it restitution, the Disney corporation has at least begun a massive restoration effort.

In 1992, Disney made an historical agreement with federal and state environmental officials. In return for its being allowed to bulldoze and develop 550 acres of wetlands during the building of its model town Celebration, Disney purchased an ecologically important preserve of 8,500 acres about 15 miles south on the Osceola-Polk county border called the Walker Ranch, and then turned it over (along with $8 million to establish a trust fund) to the Nature Conservancy for restoration and maintenance. The idea was to return the area to the condition it was in 500 years ago, before the European explorers arrived, which meant somehow reversing nearly a century of excessive drainage, clear-cutting, cattle grazing, and even turpentine distilleries. Whole sections of introduced vegetation would have to be burned, fences and roads turned under, and grasslands and swamp reintroduced.

It was a good deal for both sides. From the environmental point of view, the Walker Ranch was desirable because it held the highest concentration of nesting bald eagles in the southeast, along with stable populations of wood storks, scrub jays, herons, ibis, fox squirrels, bobcats, indigo snakes, and gopher tortoises. It also hosted rare southeastern kestrels and Audubon's crested caracara. It was a good deal for Disney because it spent less than $40 million—$20 million to the previous developer, $9 million to the Nature Conservancy for restoration and a maintenance endowment, and about $11 million for research and permit reconciliation—instead of what might have been a great deal more in wetlands construction permits and waiver hearings.

The agreement turned out to be such a public relations boon, as well as such smart development planning, that Disney World's rival, the Universal Studios park, shortly thereafter made a similar deal to restore and preserve another 270 acres that adjoined the Walker Ranch. State and federal regulators agreed, because the value of having a single large preserve is many times greater than having piecemeal wetlands constantly threatened on the margins. That deal freed Universal to begin its huge second phase alongside Interstate 4 on a tract that had included wetlands. The

Greater Orlando Aviation Authority negotiated a similar land swap in the same area.

Renamed the Disney Wilderness Preserve, and now totaling 11,000 acres, the Walker Ranch area includes piney flats, prairies, cypress swamp (home to rare Florida black bears and panthers), and bay swamp. It's also a test site for the introduction of cloned indigenous plant species, as mentioned above.

Like Discovery Island, the Wilderness Preserve has had its share of unwanted residents. Wild pigs that were rooting up delicate plants and reproducing too rapidly for ordinary control, had to be trapped and killed by security forces under reluctant Nature Conservancy orders. These were not cute Piglet types, but 400-pound crashing boors, so to speak. Besides, they weren't indigenous to the area, but 16th-century ingrates brought along by the pork-hungry Spanish. Once slaughtered, they were left to feed the raptors.

• The Park *Jurassic Park* Built •

Disney World's largest theme park would have been called the Wild Kingdom if Mutual of Omaha hadn't found that a little too close to its own famous TV show title. But when Disney's Animal Kingdom, as it is now simply known, opens in 1998, it will be five times the size of the Magic Kingdom, with a 14-story Tree of Life for a castle. It has already been the target of protests by PETA (People for the Ethical Treatment of Animals), but Disney, in a typically clever preemptive PR strike, has hired animal specialists and conservationists, and enlisted the tentative support of the ASPCA and the Florida Audubon Society for the project. The director of animal operations is Rick Barongi, former curator of mammals at the highly regarded San Diego Zoo, who says the "foundation of the park is conservation ethics."

According to the plans, it will be divided into at least three themed areas, each with some sort of thrill ride—something like a modern Adventureland, only vastly spread out. One area will be a real-life safari park, with herds of Asian and African live animals, including giraffes, hippos, and elephants, in carefully reconstructed habitats representing rain forests, plains, and savannah. The inside buzz has it that the African adventure begins when the jeep guide promises to show visitors a mammoth mother elephant named Big Red; moments later, the jeep comes upon Big Red's "corpse" and a group of poachers, who flee as the jeep approaches. A whirlwind chase ensues. But there will also be a "backstage" conservation station where visitors can learn about breeding, research, and on-site veterinary work.

Rumor also says one section may reproduce a rain forest with a river cruise—Adventureland's Jungle Cruise finally updated. If that is so, and if the Animal Kingdom opens on schedule, it would effectively blunt another Universal Studios project: the Islands of Adventure theme park, expected to open in 1999.

The Beastly Kingdom will be a mythical forest pop-

ulated by dragons, unicorns, and other fabulous creatures (the new Fantasyland); since Disney has produced
a series of remarkable dragons, from *Sleeping Beauty* to
Dragonslayer, they should be pretty impressive.

But even they will pale next to the audio-animatronic dinosaurs that will wander the ancient landscape of Dinoland, a re-creation of Cretaceous-period
Earth. More sophisticated than the prehistoric den-
izens of the Universe of Energy ride at EPCOT,
which are direct tributes to the "Rite of Spring" segment of *Fantasia,* these dinosaurs are expected to set
new standards for realism—expectations that have to
be pretty high in the era of velociraptors. (And let's be
frank: It didn't hurt Disney plans that *Jurassic Park*
was a monster hit—and that it has a sequel in the
works.) Rumor has it that the thrill ride here will cli-
max in another chase: one of the guests by T. Rex.

While clearing the 500-acre tract, Disney Development Co. unexpectedly stumbled upon some ancient animals already there. The first were gopher tortoises, unobtrusive types who dig deep burrows other
animals then move into. Though not endangered,
they are classified as a species of special concern. As
part of the Walker Ranch deal that allowed Disney to
develop its own wetlands, conservation officials also
told Disney it would be allowed to wipe out as many
as 2,300 tortoises over 20 years. However, many of
the slow-moving residents were already suffering from
an upper respiratory illness that causes runny noses,
watery eyes, and coughing. Although it sounds some-

thing like a human cold, it is more dangerous, and a similar ailment has killed large numbers of endangered desert tortoises out west. Therefore, Disney decided to give as many of the gopher tortoises as it could capture, along with $700,000 in research funds, to the University of Florida.

In 1994, Disney Development Co. found that the same area was also home to skinks, tiny lizards who lived in central Florida thousands of years ago. So it transplanted 22 acres of sand hill terrain, 6–12 inches deep, in a unique effort to re-create an entire habitat, and then repatriated 200 skinks. The 22 acres, taken to the western edge of Disney property, have been marked off into one-acre lots, in order for researchers to gauge the skinks' adaptability to other environments.

• Earth, Air, Fire, and Water •

As large a project as it was, carving out Seven Seas Lagoon was only a part of the great dredging program that building Walt Disney World required. Under natural circumstances, the Reedy Creek district would have been three-quarters inundated in the summer and one-quarter water in winter. Most of the property was at least permanently damp. So, like that other Creator, Disney World's makers first had to divide the waters from the land, and they had to make sure they stayed divided. That meant relocating 9 million cubic yards of dirt—enough to rebuild the Meadowlands sports complex in New Jersey three times over—and carving out 55 miles of canals.

The water levels then had to be regulated. At the same time, however, Imagineers had to be careful not to contaminate, concentrate, or drain away water from land that had already been disastrously over-drained in many nearby areas. The water reclamation system designed by the Imagineers involved not only the canals, but miles and miles of levees and a series of innovated water control gates—entirely mechanical in nature, so that no electrical wiring or human intrusion is required—that serve as "locks" to keep the water in the canals and rivers within desirable limits. It even restricts flooding during periods of heavy rain and hurricane weather. Since the late 1970s, the water flow has been monitored by a satellite in stationary orbit using radio telemetry.

The naturally swampy conditions continue to make life a little difficult from time to time. Pleasure Island opened a year later than originally scheduled, and its original 30-million-dollar budget nearly tripled, because the "island" kept sinking. In 1992, Disney's own environmental staff voluntarily reported to the U.S. Army Corps that just over an acre of wetlands had been inadvertently filled in during the construction of the Bonnet Creek golf course. They were fined and ordered to restore the grounds.

Incidentally, the Imagineers didn't just have to make new lakes; they had to remake Bay Lake—the little blue gem that had persuaded Walt to buy the land in the first place—by draining it, dredging the white sand clean, and refilling it. Joe Potter's engineers created tides as well, by installing a computerized wave-maker that produced a seemingly natural range of ripples from a few inches to four feet high. Just imagine what Walt would have said if he'd known that.

Nor was that the end of it. When it came time to build EPCOT, the engineers had to haul the earthmovers out of mothballs to dredge another six million cubic yards of dirt to keep the World Showcase Lagoon down—it was a massive sinkhole—and the rest of the park "up."

• The Kingdom and the Power •

Walt Disney's determination to have a spotlessly clean prototype of a park placed extra pressure on Imagineers to create an effective and virtually invisible waste management system. Part of the problem of littering was solved by reinventing the street sweeper: *Mary Poppins*–era types with long pushbrooms. (I have a special respect for these often overlooked laborers. As a small child, I got lost in Disneyland, and, remembering the "Missing Children" sign on Town Hall, I approached a street sweeper in tears asking for directions. He kindly altered his brushing route to lead me there, telling stories in character the whole way.)

The commercial trash problem in the Magic Kingdom and at the Contemporary Resort, part of the original construction, was solved by the Swedish AVAC (automated vacuum-assisted collection) system built into the Utilidor, which is capable of swallowing 50 tons a day. Disney employees take the liner bags from the trash cans to the pneumatic AVAC tubes that suck the bags in and hurl them out, at an estimated 60 miles per hour, to a central collection point. The garbage is compacted there and then trucked to a blast-furnace incinerator.

By experimenting and adjusting its methods over the years, Disney has managed to integrate some progressive methods into its wastewater management, and to integrate that with its solid waste treatment and power production as well. The sewage facility is so efficient that when the treated and chlorinated water is released, it nearly meets federal drinking water standards. Some of it is used to irrigate the golf courses and wildlife areas. Some of the treated water is used to irrigate the 150-acre Living Filter Tree Farm, which is just what it says: a natural filtration system. (The roots and sand layer absorb certain minerals from the water before it sinks through the earth back into the groundwater.) And some of the water is used to spray exhaust at the incinerator to capture ash. The ash is then recycled again through the sewage plant, where it serves as a filter, and eventually it is mixed with sludge from the sewage plant and used as fertilizer.

The Water Hyacinth Project (co-funded by the EPA, Solar Energy Research Institute, NASA, University of Florida, University of Arizona, and several other corporations) was a well-publicized experiment in using the otherwise undesirable plant to absorb organic waste in the water through its floating roots. The plants were then harvested for either composting or some sort of animal feed. However, cattle found the stuff unappetizing, and so far the processed hyacinths haven't found an ideal purpose. The program, therefore, has been suspended.

One by-product of the constant search for bigger, better, faster amusements at the park and for bigger, fancier resorts and restaurants, is that the demand for power has mushroomed. (That's not a pun, but in the late 1980s, Disney also participated in a simulated nuclear waste disposal project that was federally funded. No real "hot" waste was burned, and Disney said it agreed to help only to get rid of more ordinary garbage. But that didn't turn out to be very cost-efficient either. However, the experiment did reveal that the state charter theoretically permits Disney to own and operate a nuclear fission reactor.) The amount of power needed to run the whole park when it opened would barely maintain the Magic Kingdom today.

Walt Disney World produces approximately one-quarter of its own energy through a combination of electric generation, energy recycling, and solar energy; the rest is purchased from outside sources. The Central Energy Plant produces about 30% of the electricity, all of the hot water, and most of the air-conditioning water used in the park. It uses both gas turbine and steam turbine techniques to drive generators that can run on either diesel fuel or natural gas, whichever is less expensive at the time. (Disney had previously experimented with blast-furnace incineration using solid waste to produce steam heat, but it wasn't cost-efficient.) The steam from the turbines is then recaptured and recycled for use in heating water, running the air-conditioning system, and so on. A secondary facility at EPCOT provides chilled and warm water for that park. The newer office buildings have some solar panels, and most of the later resorts have been designed using such energy-conserving techniques as angling windows, employing natural shade, and ventilation. Power is further conserved by computers that monitor high- and low-use cycles at the park.

Even so, power is not always available on demand, especially in Florida. So what happens in a regional blackout from a hurricane or other disaster? If you're in Disney World, not much. The company has a diesel generator capable of running all critical systems in the park. And in case the natural gas pipeline is damaged, the park has more than a million gallons of diesel fuel on hand.

MICKEY & COMPANY

The Cast and Crew

*W*hat's it like to work in Wonderland? Well, like anywhere else, it has its drawbacks, but the number of employees who stay with the company for 20 and 30 years is a fair recommendation. In fact, the membership of Disneyana, a combination fan club/convention/souvenir collectors' army that convenes twice a year, includes as many current and former employees as plain ol' Mickey fans.

The real explanation seems to be that the company fosters both a sense of responsibility and a sense of fun. Every new employee, or cast member, as they are always called (even in those nonperforming departments of the company), is required to take a two-day course called "Traditions": a mix of company legend, behavioral guidelines, and psycho-social bonding. "You come out totally believing in 'The Disney Way'," said a five-year veteran. "It's almost like Walt is alive and well. It's a total immersion thing. You talk about

'Disney this' and 'Disney that': We call it getting dosed with pixie dust. It lasts about a year—and of course some people have to go through it again."

Employees also have benefits with emotionally, if not economically, addictive properties: All full-time employees get at least 12 days' free admission to the parks a year, plus free parking and access to all other World facilities, including a cast-only recreation park. Salaried employees have "silver passes," good for un- limited free access for four people. (Corporate execs carry "gold passes," good for as many people as they want to bring in.)

"This is the greatest job," said Mark Mattern of the Disney Institute's culinary school. "You get to teach people hands-on, you have state-of-the-art facilities, medical insurance, a great place to live—and I can take my kid to the Magic Kingdom any time I want." And the pay, at least according to Mattern, is com- petitive; Mattern said he was offered the job of host chef for the Atlanta Olympics, but turned it down for the Disney World job.

There are frequent organized cast functions and special events such as "Thursday night at the movies." And whenever there are new amusements or rides about to open, it's the cast members who get to play guinea pig. One woman remembered riding Splash Mountain so many times that she knew all the songs by heart—"and they kept yelling over the PR, 'Please keep your hands in the boat!' because there was a huge splash fight going on."

"Yeah, you get a little jaded working here sometimes, until you're out with somebody who's never seen the park before," agreed another cast member. "And then they go nuts and all of a sudden you think, 'Hey, I work at this place that really makes people happy!'"

• "Pixie Dust" •

If all those Japanese-style training manuals had been published 40 years ago, you'd think Disney had read them. When it comes to in-house behavior, Disney has little interest in self-expression. The training phases of Disney employment is just as exhaustively detailed as the planning, zoning, paint colors, and wallpaper at the Castle.

In fact, "Traditions" is being exported to outside companies, just as some management groups invited Japanese executives in during the '80s. (*In Search of Excellence* author, Tom Peters, cited "Traditions" as one of the best such indoctrination programs in 1982.) The Disney University has turned some Disney Way rules into a shakedown seminar for managers that, for example, persuaded one public hospital to set up a "back stage" for the staff, where they could relax from the stress of emergency treatment and even death. Others package management skills. Another group of professional development courses are designed specifically for educators, to show them ways of adapting marketing and motivation techniques to the classroom.

These professional services are being aggressively promoted at a time when many corporations are thinning out exactly the middle-level managers who might have run such programs. Among graduating "classes" of the university have been employees of the CIA, Burger King and McDonald's, and Coke and Pepsi. The three-day programs cost about $2,000 per person, and mini-seminars are available for business conventions and special meetings.

The business and technical training at Walt Disney World has become so proficient that college students can work on-site for credits in business, human resources, retailing, food and beverage management, and so on. More than 3,000 13-week interns take part in this hands-on training every year. (In typical pixie dust style, graduates can earn either "Mouster's" or "Ducktorate" degrees.) There are also full-term internships available through the corporations that sponsor the various pavilions.

Working at Disney World does not suit everybody. One man who got a summer job as a character role was busted almost immediately for improvising and was exiled to an ice cream stand. "I was just part of a machine that operated exactly the same way, paraded at exactly the same time, orchestrated by other machines . . . and all for minimum wage." He stayed only a few weeks.

But the company is very up-front about its requirements. In the first rather sketchy interview, prospective employees are told about the dress code, the likelihood that they'll be working on holidays, which are especially busy park days, and so on. Only if they accept these basic requirements are they scheduled for in-depth interviews. Those who will be in contact with the public are interviewed in small groups, so that they have to interact; craft workers are evaluated one-on-one by their professional peers (which is also true of prospective Disney Institute faculty).

With rare exceptions, the rules have remained unchanged for 40 years, since the opening of Disneyland: no ad-libbing, no fraternizing, no obvious makeup, except in character. Cast members, costumed or not, are required to look as squeaky-clean as the original Mouseketeers (and with haircuts for men almost as short as Spin and Marty's): no facial hair for men (which includes sideburns) or hair that covers the shirt collar, but no shaved heads either; no visible tattoos; no nose or other piercing except for the ear lobe, and only two earring holes—and only for women; no obvious bralessness; no bright nail polish or excessively long nails; and no excess jewelry.

Those cast members chosen to portray the cartoon characters such as Mickey and Minnie, called "greeters" because they interact with the public, must never speak. (Any Mouse-loving kid would immediately know it was the "wrong" voice.) Those who do speak must stick to the script; improvisation is allowed in only very specific situations. Even the professionals and adult-education instructors, who work face-to-face with visitors, still find their new, looser public-relations rules confusing: "I never thought in 25 years I'd be talking with a guest, much less out drinking with her."

It's against the rules to be seen wearing your costume anywhere but in your assigned area, so all cast members must begin and end every shift by changing clothes. Because no one is allowed to take the costumes home or to sleep on park grounds, employees who have a late shift followed by an early one may find their off hours quite abbreviated. Many of the costumes are heavy and hot, and some that have limited vision and restricted movements can be painful and even hazardous. Characters say that a surprising number of children, and even some adults, want to punch or kick them or trip them.

Even behind the scenes, few things are as they seem. Considering the costume requirements, many of the cast members chosen for most "greeter" parts have to be fairly small. "They're just very little people," said a taller co-worker. "And Mickey's actually a girl— which gets weird when she starts kissing people."

There is one other fantastic quality of Walt Disney World, and you may not have noticed it yet: Nobody is allowed to die here. This is a lesson cast members have to learn early on. Of course, it's a matter of perception, not reality: with hundreds of thousands of visitors every day, Disney World's daily population is larger than many cities in the country, and sheer statistical probability means that every once in a while, a guest will pass into the great Adventureland. But not on stage—not if the cast members can help it. Employees tell very hushed stories about having to pass off corpses as drunks or victims of ordinary trippings. In a fairly notorious case, a man jumped from the top-floor restaurant of the Contemporary Resort into the atrium, and there were shell-shocked staffers mumbling, "He's okay, he'll be fine, just a moment, please."

As an employer, Disney has some progressive attitudes, including some that are implicit proof of change. Only a few years ago, a gay couple sued Disney World because they had been prevented from dancing together; these days, the company extends insurance benefits to same-sex partners, for example (at least a tacit acknowledgment that many of its own employees are gay); and gay and lesbian groups have convened at Walt Disney World for a long weekend for several years, partying and parading.

A bus driver described his job as being a model of flexibility: He can work either four 10-hour days or five 8-hour shifts, has regular breaks, and, depending on his seniority, could work his way into the shift times he preferred.

Walt Disney World also has some very corporate attitudes. It is the state's, and the region's, largest employer, even when it isn't in the midst of major construction. In relatively quiet times, it employs 33,000 people full-time and about 6,000 part-time—not just the 200 or so Mickeys and Cinderellas but the guides at the rides, the street sweepers, animal-care specialists, food and beverage workers, camera technicians, computer programmers, agriculturalists, life-guards, makeup artists, the maintenance workers who paint the Carrousel every night, and the ones who sew up ripped costumes every day. In another few years, with the opening of Animal Kingdom and additional resort areas, it expects to increase both part- and full-time positions by several thousand each.

But that also means increased labor costs, and a couple of years ago, faced with billion-dollar labor costs, the company decided that employees should share the costs of health care premiums that had always been free. Management also decided to try to use more part-time workers, who are not covered by contracts; reduce benefits for full-time employees; and hire outside contractors more frequently. The renegotiations were drawn-out and often quite acrimonious.

Eventually the unions ratified a package of five health-care plans and 3–4% raises. It also required that those employees who were replaced by contract labor be found full-time jobs within the company.

Despite the long impasse, the pixie dust stuck. Except for a few "street-theater" demonstrations against the company, the esprit de corps remained unusually high. A character actor, who had complained at humorous length about the weight of his costume on a hot day, wound up saying, "But it sure beats sitting at a desk all day."

Even cast members who have had bad experiences tend to find ways to excuse the corporation. Two women chefs, who said they'd been looked down on or ridiculed in the kitchens, attributed the bias to the culinary culture rather than the Disney Way. "I can't say we didn't have problems getting positions of power, but that's the usual problem of being a girl in a kitchen full of boys. Only a few executive chefs are women."

As one woman who has been employed by and quit the company several times said, "I still love the place. I hope to go back. For all its problems, I still feel a great deal of loyalty to it, and I wouldn't like to see a bad book written about it."

As mentioned in "The Mouse That Scored," everybody, even CEO Michael Eisner, is on a first-name basis. Even official nametags are printed only with first names. (And those, according to recent offers, are worth at least $25 on the Disneyana black market.) "After eight years, I can go anywhere on the property and know somebody. Of course, I may only know his first name," a cast member joked.

Disney prefers to hire from within for management positions, because they can be sure that the employees understand the operation and support it. Opportunities to move up, or just into different areas of the corporation, are posted in the cast center and circulated in in-house newsletters. (Applicants are re-interviewed, retrained, and sometimes re-"dusted" as well.) Younger employees are often reminded that there are many executives in the company who started out at very menial levels—most famously Dick Nunis, the one-time Disneyland dishwasher, who was head of operations during the construction of Walt Disney World and wound up being president of both U.S. amusement parks. Eisner himself started out as a page, although at NBC.

The stories are a little misleading, perhaps. Nunis, for example, though he is still a corporate vice-president, was eased out of real power some years ago. A highly placed Orlando businessman says that Eisner realized that Nunis's sometimes truculent style was not improving Disney's public image. Fewer managers who have fallen short of expectations are given second chances in other departments, which was standard procedure in the old days. And with the increased emphasis on public access in the park, on showing off the serious science and conservation efforts being made, and on the professional classes at the Disney Institute, a greater number of staffers with traditional credentials are needed.

Still, cast members say they are constantly encouraged to look into management openings as well as on- or off-stage jobs. Periodic evaluations of staff prospects allow supervisors to maintain a sense of their employees' hopes and their likely professional fit; employees who don't do well in one area are given second chances in other departments. The Disney company has unusually low employee turnover.

The foreign pavilions at EPCOT's World Showcase, and even a few of the exotic attractions elsewhere, require foreign cast members. Consequently, the company has set up a "World College" extension program that recruits international cast members and gets them cultural exchange visas. But Disney takes its responsibility as "host family" very seriously. The exchange students are the only cast members who actually live on campus, in a community called Vista Way that is run as strictly as an old-style college dorm—no mixed-sex apartment mates and strict security check-ins. The major problem the World College has, cast members say, is that none of the students ever want to go home.

Uncle Scrooge

Remember that not all Disney features were commercial successes the first time around. Remember also that animation was still an unformed creature, shedding its skin, growing feathers; and that it was a brainstorm of Walt's to withdraw the features from circulation and only periodically (every seven years—just long enough to develop a new audience) to re-release them.

The fact remains that a surprising number of the live actors who gave voice (or music) to some of the biggest cartoon hits in the Disney stable had to sue the company to get their fair share of the proceeds. And oddly enough, Disney seems willing to risk losing face by taking on some of the best known faces, or voices, in the business.

One less-attractive aspect of Disney corporate behavior is its occasional tone of "it's not personal, it's business." Even, sometimes, when it comes to old friends. The Philadelphia Orchestra, which not only provided the background but whose members actually appeared with maestro Leopold Stokowski in the first segments of *Fantasia,* sued for royalties when the video was released; Disney settled.

Peggy Lee, who co-wrote and sang a half-dozen songs for the 1955 *Lady and the Tramp,* sued for what she said was $10 million in unpaid video royalties; a jury awarded her about a third of what she asked. Mary Losta, the voice of Sleeping Beauty, and Ilene Woods Shaunessey, the voice of Cinderella, have followed suit. There was a long struggle with Jim Henson over a licensing agreement that Disney said allowed it to put a Muppets show into Disney-MGM Studios; the suits and countersuits became quite acrimonious before they were settled. (Ironically, Disney-MGM Studios' chairman Jeffrey Katzenberg, who later filed suit against the Disney Company himself, had frowned on the Henson-Disney battle, telling reporters that in fighting so many lawsuits, the Disney Co. "ran the risk of creating the impression that Disney has become a lot less friendly.")

The most puzzling case involved former cast member Daryan Faerve, who in 1987 suggested the company package little tubes of "pixie dust"—in this case, colored sparkling dust—as souvenirs. Faerve was told, in effect, thanks but no thanks; four months later, Disney itself began marketing just such a souvenir. Since Faerve had obtained state and federal trademark protection, he eventually settled with the company for $100,000. But as one slightly embarrassed cast member commented, "It's amazing they hadn't already thought of it—but it's even worse they tried to screw their own guy."

Disney has also been accused of taking itself and its trademarks far too seriously. It once ordered the removal of a Disney character from the side of a garbage truck because the image it conveyed apparently wasn't elevated enough. In 1989, it forced a preschool center to paint over a mural of Disney characters. (Universal promptly offered to paint a new Flintstones mural for free.) The same year, the Disney Co. threatened to sue the Academy of Movie Arts and Sciences because a skit on the annual Oscars telecast featured Tom Cruise dancing with Snow White, an engagement Disney apparently felt might damage her, well, snow-white reputation. Only after the Academy formally apologized did Disney withdraw, although by then the whole situation had been chewed over by dozens of comics and commentators.

On the other hand, those human stars who have been gathered unto the Disney fold in more recent years get not only top billing but repeat roles. Robin Williams, who appears as his animated self in the Disney-MGM Studio tour and his audio-animatronic self in Tomorrowland's *Timekeeper,* is clearly the Jiminy Cricket of the '90s—and Walter Cronkite, the "other" Uncle Walt. Martin Short and Jeremy Irons pop up repeatedly, as do Whoopi Goldberg and comic Ellen DeGeneres, star of the revised Universe of Energy show and of a Disney-produced TV sitcom.

Then there are the difficulties with cast members who take advantage of Disney rather than the other way around. In 1996, a one-day adult pass to the Magic Kingdom, EPCOT, or Disney-MGM Studios cost a little over $40; a four-day pass for one day in each park plus a "wild card," was about $135; and a four-day pass good for any park anytime cost about $200. Other big tickets include length-of-stay passes (about $300 for ten days), annual passes ($250 for the three theme parks, with a yearly $225 renewal), and World-wide annual passes that include the water parks and Pleasure Island (nearly $350 with a $300 renewal fee).

Obviously, park passes are big moneymakers, which makes them tempting targets for thieves and counterfeiters. Some of them are even cast members.

In 1994, a Disney employee took 1.75 million dollars' worth of tickets from a company vault and sold them for $200,000. The Disney employee was caught, but his accomplice was not. Net loss: a million and a half. In 1988, another employee just stuffed his pockets with tickets and took them home; he was caught and ordered to pay $58,000, but that was only a little more than half the estimated value of the tickets. And in 1993, three workers at Disney-MGM Studios worked out a ticket-upgrade scam that cost the company more than $400,000.

AFTERWORD

"Mirror, Mirror, on the Wall . . ."

*I*n the forests of eastern Volusia County, not far from where Walt Disney's parents were married, there is a nearly full-scale replica of the cottage in which Snow White lived with the Seven Dwarfs. Built along Spruce Creek and using original celluloids as carpenter's blueprints (with only these two-dimensional guidelines, the builder had to see the movie several times and then eye the proportions), it was the dream cottage of an old friend of Disney's named Judge Alfred Nippert, the son-in-law of soap magnate James Gamble. It was built in 1938, the year after the movie was released and nearly two decades before Disneyland. When Walt himself toured it, he was so touched that he sent the man full-sized dolls of Snow White and all seven friends.

The princess lay in a glass coffin in the living room. The fireplace mantel was whole timber; the heavy Gothic doors had iron strap hinges; and original cels from the movie hung around the walls. It was a perfect Black Forest fantasy, except that most of the wood was Florida cypress. Outside were lavish gardens with stone walkways, a witch's hut, a mine shaft, a wishing well, a rock garden, a garden pool built of fieldstone with a lion's head fountain, "stalagmites" of cypress knees, and statues of dwarfs and animals. It was open for tours into the '50s, when it fell into disrepair. It was rediscovered and restored a few years ago using historic photographs and is now part of the Gamble Place history and education center operated by the Daytona Beach Museum of Arts and Sciences.

There are photos of the judge, pipe in hand, rocking in one of the cypress chairs he had built for the place. It's almost irresistible to imagine that he retreated to the cottage as a refuge from the intricacies of judicial rhetoric—that he longed for a world in which good and evil were so clearly opposed, and so totally vanquished. But even more, it's sweet to think that such an august professional knew, with as much affection as any small child, the names of those magnificent seven: Sneezy, Sleepy, Happy, Dopey, Grumpy, Bashful, and Doc.

When astronaut Sally Ride was asked to describe her journey into space, she called it "an E-ticket ride." In the early days, Disneyland and Disney World both used an ornate system of ticket books. "A" tickets were for "A" rides, "B" tickets for "B" attractions, and so on. The most elaborate attractions required the expensive "E" tickets, so Ride was really saying the launch had lived up to her wildest childhood fantasies.

How many of us can honestly say we have never been touched by Walt Disney's dream? wouldn't love to fly, stay young forever, slay the dragon, or become a real live person? Maybe that's what still makes Walt Disney World fascinating—not its technological wizardry, but the simple wonder at its heart. Overshadowed though the Magic Kingdom may be by the newer attractions, it remains Walt's real World, and his great gift to us. Maybe it is only an imitation paradise, but if we don't have models to go by, how will we remember—in this exhausting, selfish, violent, and often soul-crushing world—that there was ever a star to wish on? If a child does not say, "I believe, I do believe," how much darker and narrower will his future be? If she does not learn to love A Bear of Very Little Brain, how will she learn to hear the inarticulate sufferers of the world?

I believe in the power of imagination. I believe in the unexplored possibilities of the spirit. And I believe that the heart, like any other muscle, grows stiff if it is not exercised regularly.

I believe.

APPENDIX

A BRIEF HISTORY
OF THE WORLD

1961

Encouraged by the phenomenal success of Disneyland in Anaheim, California, Walt Disney en-
visions a second theme park located somewhere
in the eastern United States.

1962

As Disney formulates plans for his eastern park, he
focuses on four essential prerequisites:

1. The park must be located in a temperate
   climate that allows year-round operation.

2. Enough land must be acquired to insulate the
   park from the sort of crass commercialism and
   conflicting environment that enveloped
   Disneyland.

3. Disney must have absolute autonomy and
   authority in the development of the new property and must be essentially exempt from
   development covenants, building codes, and
   other local restrictions.

4. State and county government must commit to providing necessary infrastructure (highways, etc.) to support the Disney project.

1963

Because of its weather and commitment to tourism, Florida is selected as the best location for the new park.

The search bypasses coastal areas to focus on the Orlando area, where large expanses of land are available at bargain prices. Orlando is also situated at the crossroads of Florida's primary traffic arteries.

The concept for the new park first expands to become a complete destination resort and then subsequently enlarges to become EPCOT, the Experimental Prototype Community of Tomorrow. According to Walt Disney's vision, the entire development known as EPCOT would contain a Disneyland clone theme park, hotels, lakes, highways, recreation areas, and a futuristic utopian city populated initially by Disney employees.

Negotiations begin with the State of Florida for tax concessions, local jurisdictional waivers, and infra-structure commitments.

1964

Using a number of agents, Disney clandestinely begins acquiring land. Ultimately, 28,000 acres

are acquired from more than 100 property owners
at an average cost of about $200 per acre.

1965

Though the project is first exposed by the *Orlando
Sentinel*, the official announcement is made on
November 16, at a press conference with Walt
Disney, his brother Roy Disney, and Florida
Governor Hayden Burns. Walt Disney shares his
expectation that the vacation destination would
evolve to become a utopian community offering
a way of life that marries the values of turn-of-
the-century America with the technology of the
future.

1966

Detailed planning of the Florida Disney project
continues until the death of Walt Disney in
December.

1967

After Walt's death, Roy Disney, Donn B. Tatum, and
E. Cardon Walker, the company's top executives,
carry the project forward, but begin to diverge from
Walt's vision. Site preparation begins. Swamps and
wetlands are reclaimed through the development of
a system of water-control channels.

1968

Legislation is passed creating the Reedy Creek
Development District, a veritable state within a

state. The legislation allows Disney to develop its
28,000 acres without interference from Orange
and Osceola counties.

1969

Construction begins on "Phase I," to include the
Magic Kingdom, the Contemporary Resort, the
Polynesian Resort, Fort Wilderness Campground,
two 18-hole golf courses, and the Disney
Transportation System. The target date for the
opening is October 1, 1971.

1970

Construction continues, including the creation of the
Seven Seas Lagoon, a 200-acre lake fronting the
Magic Kingdom that connects to Bay Lake by
canal.

1971

Construction clips along at a frantic pace as the opening date approaches. Before the gates open, the
project will have involved approximately 9,000
workers and cost $400 million.

During all of September, while finishing touches are
applied, more than 100,000 Disney employees
and local guests preview the project.

On October 1, Walt Disney World opens to the public. The William Windsor family is the first to
enter.

A gala grand opening is staged on October 23–25,

with Arthur Fiedler conducting the World
Symphony Orchestra. The Magic Kingdom's
opening parade features a 1,076-piece marching
band with 76 trombones à la the *Music Man.*

Circle-Vision 360's *America the Beautiful* opens in
November, followed by Flight to the Moon in
December.

The attendance record for 1971 is set on December
29, when 69,500 guests tour the Magic Kingdom.

1972

If You Had Wings opens in Tomorrowland.

Six additional monorail trains and two ferry boats are
brought on line.

Attendance totals just under 11 million guests for the
first complete year of operation (almost exactly
the same first-year total registered by Euro
Disneyland 20 years later).

72,000-plus guests visit the Magic Kingdom on
December 27, setting a new one-day record.

1973

The Golf Resort Hotel (later called the Disney Inn)
opens. The quietest and most adult of all Disney
lodging properties, the hotel was leased to the
Department of Defense and renamed Shades of
Green in 1994.

Pirates of the Caribbean opens in New Orleans
Square.

The Walt Disney Story premiers on Main Street.

The Swan Boats open on the drawbridge side of
Cinderella Castle.

Tom Sawyer Island begins operations in Frontierland.

The Richard F. Irvine Steamboat is launched in
Liberty Square.

Another one-day attendance record is set on April 17,
when over 73,000 guests visit the park.

Walt Disney Productions celebrates its 50th
anniversary.

Richard Nixon is a guest at the Contemporary
Resort.

Construction gets underway on Space Mountain in
Tomorrowland.

1974

StarJets begin service in Tomorrowland.

Discovery Island, a bird sanctuary in Bay Lake, opens
to the public.

At the Fort Wilderness Campground, the Pioneer
Hall dinner theater opens.

Donald Duck turns 40.

On December 27, 74,600 guests pass through the
Magic Kingdom turnstiles, setting a new one-day
attendance record.

1975

Space Mountain opens in January.

Also in Tomorrowland, the GE *Carousel of Progress* begins its long tenure at Walt Disney World. The attraction had originally been designed by Disney for the 1964 New York World's Fair.

The WEDway PeopleMover comes on line in Tomorrowland.

An updated *America the Beautiful* premiers at Circle-Vision 360.

Mission to Mars replaces Flight to the Moon.

The Lake Buena Vista Shopping Village (later the Walt Disney World Village Marketplace) opens in March.

Plans for EPCOT are revealed and differ significantly from Walt Disney's original concept.

Two single-day attendance records are set at the Magic Kingdom: 82,300 guests on March 25 and then 82,400 guests on New Years Eve.

1976

The River Country water park opens adjacent to the Fort Wilderness Campground.

The Magic Kingdom welcomes its 50-millionth visitor in March.

1977

The *Empress Lilly* Riverboat restaurant (named for Walt Disney's wife) is dedicated at the Lake Buena Vista Shopping Village.

The Main Street Electrical Parade premiers at the Magic Kingdom.

A new one-day attendance record is set on December 28, as almost 83,000 guests tour the Magic Kingdom.

1978

Mickey Mouse celebrates his 50th birthday.

Opening for EPCOT is targeted for 1982.

One-day attendance breaks the 85,000-guest threshold on March 28.

1979

Construction begins on Big Thunder Mountain Railroad.

Construction begins on EPCOT Center.

The Magic Kingdom receives its 100-millionth visitor on October 22, almost eight years exactly from the date of the park's grand opening.

1980

Big Thunder Mountain Railroad opens in Frontierland.

The old single-day attendance record is shattered when 93,000 guests inundate the Magic Kingdom on New Year's Eve.

Construction continues on EPCOT Center and on a new monorail loop connecting the Transportation and Ticket Center to EPCOT Center.

1981

Broadway at the Top dinner show opens at the Top of the World restaurant at the Contemporary Resort.

Construction continues at EPCOT Center.

1982

EPCOT Center opens to the public on October 1. Completely transformed by corporate Disney, EPCOT Center is a theme park as opposed to the working, prototypical community that Walt Disney envisioned.

The grand opening was covered by over 1,000 print and broadcast journalists.

1983

Walt Disney World's 150-millionth visitor arrives on April 11.

New World Fantasy, a fireworks, fountains, and laser precursor to *IllumiNations,* debuts on the World Showcase Lagoon at EPCOT Center.

1984

Donald Duck celebrates his 50th birthday.

The Moroccan pavilion opens in the World Showcase section of EPCOT Center.

A new movie, *American Journeys,* debuts at Circle-Vision 360 in Tomorrowland.

The Big Thunder Shooting Gallery opens in Frontierland.

1985

Responding to an earlier announcement by Universal Studios, Disney unveils plans for the Disney-MGM Studios Tour.

At the Magic Kingdom, Tinkerbell's Flight is added to the Fantasy in the Sky fireworks spectacular.

A daytime show featuring airplanes, kites, and speedboats premiers on the World Showcase Lagoon at EPCOT Center.

1986

The Living Seas opens in the Future World section of EPCOT Center.

Captain EO replaces *Magic Journeys* at the Magic Eye Theater at the Journey into Imagination pavilion at EPCOT Center. *Magic Journeys* reappears in the Magic Kingdom.

Construction gets underway for the Disney-MGM Studios, the Grand Floridian Beach Resort, the Norway pavilion at EPCOT Center, and Pleasure Island, a nightlife entertainment complex.

1987

Walt Disney World's 250-millionth visitor arrives. Attendance at Walt Disney World passes the official population of the United States.

In Disney's version of an Elvis impersonator convention, all of the cast members who played Snow

White during the Magic Kingdom's first 15 years gathered for a reunion.

The Disney Information Center off I-75 in Ocala opens.

With the introduction of Disney Dollars, Disney begins printing and issuing its own currency.

1988

IllumiNations debuts.

Construction begins on the Wonders of Life pavilion at EPCOT Center.

Mickey's Birthdayland, the first new land in the Magic Kingdom, opens in celebration of Mickey Mouse's 60th birthday. Attractions include a stop on the Walt Disney World Railroad, Mickey's House, a stage show presentation of a surprise birthday party, and a chance to meet Mickey in his dressing room for photos.

The Norway pavilion at EPCOT Center opens, featuring Maelstrom, an indoor boat ride.

The Grand Floridian Resort opens.

The Caribbean Beach Resort brings the first third of its rooms on line.

1989

Disney-MGM Studios opens May 1, almost two years ahead of rival Universal Studios Florida. Attendance at the new park exceeds expectations and requires enlargement of the parking lot.

Typhoon Lagoon, a water theme park featuring slides and a surf pool, opens June 1.

Pleasure Island opens in late June as a gated attraction with six nightclubs.

Disney and Delta Airlines convert *If You Had Wings* (in Tomorrowland) to Dreamflight.

The Wonders of Life pavilion opens in the Future World section of EPCOT Center. Feature attractions include Body Wars and Cranium Command.

1990

Star Tours opens at the Disney-MGM Studios.

Honey, I Shrunk the Kids Movie Set Adventure, a children's playground, debuts at the Disney-MGM Studios.

Here Come the Muppets, a stage show featuring the Muppet characters, kicks off a two-year run at the Studios.

Also at the Studios, Disney launches Sorcery in the Sky fireworks.

The Teenage Mutant Ninja Turtles are added to the live entertainment mix at the Studios.

Mickey's Birthdayland at the Magic Kingdom becomes Mickey's Starland. A new character show featuring characters from the Disney cable channel premiers.

The Walt Disney World Swan and the Walt Disney World Dolphin resorts open near EPCOT Center.

The International Gateway opens, providing a direct entrance into EPCOT Center through the World Showcase section of the park.

Disney Yacht Club Resort and Disney Beach Club Resort open. Both resorts are within walking distance of the new International Gateway to EPCOT Center.

1991

Jim Henson's *MuppetVision 3-D* opens at the Disney-MGM Studios.

Sci-Fi Dine-In Theater initiates service at the Studios.

The SpectroMagic parade replaces the Main Street Electrical Parade in the Magic Kingdom.

The Port Orleans Resort opens.

1992

Walt Disney World records its 400-millionth guest.

Splash Mountain opens in Frontierland at the Magic Kingdom.

The Studios launch a new parade based on the Disney animated feature *Aladdin.*

Legend of the Little Mermaid, a theater presentation, debuts at the Disney-MGM Studios.

Disney's Dixie Landings Resort opens in January.

Disney begins selling memberships in the Disney Vacation Club Resort, a time-share development.

The Osprey Ridge and Eagle Pine golf courses open at Disney's Bonnet Creek Golf Club.

1993

The American Adventure in the World Showcase section of EPCOT Center is renovated.

In the Magic Kingdom, the *Carousel of Progress* in Tomorrowland is updated. To the consternation of some and the joy of others, the "Now Is the Best Time" theme song is scrapped.

The Hall of Presidents is also made current with the addition of President Bill Clinton.

Splashtacular and *The Magical World of Barbie* (the doll) are added to the live entertainment schedule at EPCOT Center.

The Walt Disney Story on Main Street is closed. Go figure.

1994

Mary Smith of Decatur, Illinois, becomes the 1-billionth guest to visit a Disney theme park.

EPCOT Center changes its name to EPCOT '94. Later the "94" is dropped.

The Land pavilion in the Future World section of EPCOT is renovated. *Kitchen Kaberet* is replaced by *Food Rocks*. The Listen to the Land boat ride is modified and renamed Living With the Land.

Innoventions, a corporate-sponsored showcase of

new products and technologies, replaces Communicore in the Future World section of EPCOT.

Honey, I Shrunk the Audience replaces *Captain EO* at the Journey into Imagination pavilion in the Future World section of EPCOT.

Spaceship Earth (the attraction in the geodesic sphere) is updated.

Horizons, in the Future World section of EPCOT, is closed when no corporate sponsor can be found.

In Tomorrowland at the Magic Kingdom, Mission to Mars closes.

Legend of the Lion King, a stage show, premiers in Fantasyland at the Magic Kingdom.

Also at the Magic Kingdom, Snow White's Adventures is upgraded. Snow White makes an appearance in the attraction for the first time in its 23-year history.

Transportarium, a Circle-Vision 360 attraction designed for Euro Disneyland, premiers in Tomorrowland at the Magic Kingdom.

The Mickey Mania parade kicks off in the Magic Kingdom.

Sunset Boulevard debuts. A major addition to the Disney-MGM Studios, the Sunset Boulevard area contains attractions, food, and shops.

"The Twilight Zone" Tower of Terror opens at the Disney-MGM Studios.

The Theater of the Stars is relocated to a more spacious quarters on Sunset Boulevard.

The Back Lot Stage opens, providing the Disney-
MGM Studios with another outdoor production
venue.

Disney's All-Star Sports Resort opens.

Disney's Wilderness Lodge opens.

Planet Hollywood opens at Pleasure Island.

1995

A total renovation of Tomorrowland in the Magic
Kingdom is completed.

Alien Encounter opens in Tomorrowland.

The RocketJets in Tomorrowland are re-themed and
called the AstroOrbiter.

The PeopleMover is renamed the Tomorrowland
Transit Authority.

In Fantasyland, 20,000 Leagues Under the Sea closes.

Blizzard Beach, the third Disney water park, opens.

The Jazz Club is added to Pleasure Island's nighttime
club scene.

Disney's All-Star Music Resort opens.

The Disney Vacation Club changes its name to
Disney's Old Key West Resort.

Disney announces plans to build a fourth major
theme park, this time with a zoological theme.

1996

The Disney Institute opens, offering a variety of life-
enriching educational experiences.

A renovation and expansion of the Walt Disney World Village Marketplace is completed.

Disney's Boardwalk Resort, offering lodging, restaurants, and entertainment, opens opposite the Yacht and Beach Club resorts.

Fantasia Gardens Miniature Golf opens near the EPCOT resort hotels.

Disney kicks off Walt Disney World's 25th anniversary party by disguising Cinderella Castle as a huge cake.

Mickey's Starland is converted to Mickey's Toontown Fair. Minnie Mouse's House, Donald Duck's boat, and a mini roller coaster are added.

Alien Encounter in Tomorrowland is closed, then reopened in a scarier version.

In Future World at EPCOT, It's Fun to Be Free, the ride at the World of Motion pavilion, closes to make way for Test Track, a new thrill ride.

Also in Future World, the Universe of Energy is updated.

Disney announces the Village Entertainment District, a 70-acre shopping, restaurant, and nightlife complex to be located near Pleasure Island.

INDEX